10.00 EC

STATE AND LOCAL ADMINISTRATION
OF
SCHOOL TRANSPORTATION

BY
ROE LYELL JOHNS, PH.D.

145047

BUREAU OF PUBLICATIONS
Teachers College, Columbia University
NEW YORK CITY
1928

Library of Congress Cataloging in Publication Data

Johns, Roe Lyell, 1900–
    State and local administration of school transporta-
tion.

    Reprint of the 1928 ed., issued in series: Teachers
College, Columbia University. Contributions to education,
no. 330.
    Originally presented as the author's thesis, Columbia.
    Bibliography: p.
    1.   School children--Transportation--United States.
2.   Education--United States--Finance. 3.   State
aid to education--United States. I.   Title.
II.   Series: Columbia University. Teachers College.
Contributions to education, no. 330.
LB2864.J6 1972   371.8'7   76-176911
ISBN 0-404-55330-3

Reprinted by Special Arrangement with Teachers
College Press, New York, New York

From the edition of 1928, New York
First AMS edition published in 1972
Manufactured in the United States

AMS PRESS, INC.
NEW YORK, N. Y.   10003

ACKNOWLEDGMENTS

The writer wishes to express his appreciation of the stimulating influence and constructive criticism of the chairman of his dissertation committee, Professor Paul R. Mort, whose previous work made possible the development of the problem. He is deeply indebted to the inspirational guidance of a man who never lost faith in him, Professor N. L. Engelhardt. He is grateful to Professor George D. Strayer for coöperation and advice in the securing of data, to Professor Carter Alexander for personal inspiration, to Professor H. A. Ruger for statistical aid, to Dr. R. L. Burns for unselfish coöperation, and to a classmate, H. R. Halsey, for valuable mathematical assistance.

Finally, the writer is most deeply indebted to his parents, whose devotion and sacrifices have made his work possible.

R. L. J.

CONTENTS

PLATES

FORMS

STATE AND LOCAL ADMINISTRATION
OF
SCHOOL TRANSPORTATION

CHAPTER I

SIGNIFICANCE OF THE CONSOLIDATION AND TRANSPORTATION MOVEMENT

EXTENT OF PROGRAM

The transportation of school children at public expense in the United States has grown from practically nothing in 1869, when Massachusetts passed the first act of authorization, to an estimated total expenditure of nearly $40,000,000 for the transportation of approximately 1,500,000 children in 1926-1927.[1]

This expenditure is approximately 2.5 per cent of the current expenditure for public schools for that year. Every state in the Union is doing some transportation, but Table I shows that more is being done in proportion to the population in the Pacific States than in any other section of the country as is indicated by the number of motor buses.

TABLE 1

NUMBER OF SCHOOL BUSES IN USE IN VARIOUS SECTIONS OF THE UNITED STATES IN 1926–1927*

Section	School Buses per 100,000 Inhabitants	Population per School Bus
United States	31.0	3,225
New England	23.7	4,229
Northeast	24.5	4,091
Southeast	39.0	2,564
Northwest	36.8	2,722
Southwest	29.6	3,377
Pacific	50.4	1,988

* Published by permission of *Bus Transportation*, McGraw-Hill Book Company, Inc., New York City.

[1] Estimations based on data furnished in *Bulletin No. 22, 1925*, United States Bureau of Education, and *Bus Transportation*, February, 1928, McGraw-Hill Publishing Company, Inc., New York City.

All of the states have laws of one sort or another that make possible the transportation of pupils at public expense.[2] Forty-three states have specific legal provisions for transportation, and in five states—Delaware, Florida, New Mexico, Utah and Wyoming—transportation of pupils at public expense is considered legal under general statutory provisions.

CAUSE OF MOVEMENT

What has caused the American public to accept transportation as a legitimate part of the expenditures for public education? Children have been transported to school, both public and private, in the United States probably from the time schools were established. It was a familiar sight to see horses hitched to the trees surrounding log schoolhouses in pioneer days. Moreover, thousands of children are still transported to school by their parents and at their expense. But every year more and more of the burden of transportation is being assumed by the school. This is due to several factors. Some of these factors will be discussed briefly.

One of the criteria of whether an activity should be supported by public taxation or not is that, if that activity can be done more efficiently at public expense than private expense, it is a legitimate part of the community's tax program. This, in effect, is coöperative action in the performance of tasks which it is necessary for many individuals to perform. The good business sense of the American people soon detected the difficulties that would arise if each family was to furnish its own conveyance, and they coöperated privately in the transportation of their children, one conveyance being used to transport the children of several families. With the increase of centralization and consolidation of schools, the next logical step was for the community as a whole to assume the burden of transportation.

Closely paralleling the growth in school transportation is the growth in consolidation of schools. It was the early ambition of every pioneer community to have a school within walking distance of every child if possible. One-room schools were built by the thousands. But in the latter quarter of the nineteenth century, this movement came to an end and communities with schools already organized began to coöperate in their endeavor to educate their children by centralization. An early evidence

[2] *Leaflet, No. 8, 1922*, Bureau of Education, Washington, D. C.

of this was the passage of an act in 1869 by the Massachusetts legislature making it possible for communities to tax themselves for the transportation of pupils. Many communities were thus enabled to take their children to a type of educational offering superior to that which they were able to afford by their own resources.

From 1917-1918 to 1921-1922, approximately 20,000 small schools were either abandoned or made centralized schools.[3] There was an elimination of about 4,500 one-room rural schools a year. Recent trends indicate that this movement has continued up to the present time.

PHILOSOPHICAL IMPLICATIONS

This movement, however, has not been accomplished and is not being carried on without serious opposition and mistrust both by the people of the community and by educational leaders. Some of the fundamental issues of political, social, and educational philosophy are involved in the question of centralization of schools. Much of the opposition has been born of sincere conviction and much of it has arisen from local jealousies and blind prejudice or sentimentality.

Chief, perhaps, among the reasons why consolidation is opposed sincerely is the fear of the dangers of centralization. The belief of thousands of people that the local community should be left with the maximum of local responsibility in all public activities has caused much fear and distrust of the concentration of schools with its consequent relinquishment of local control. Those favoring concentration of schools affirm that they, too, believe in local self-government, but they wish to define the local unit in larger terms. Those opposed to concentration of power fear that every step in that direction means a loss of local interest in that activity with a consequent trend toward bureaucratic control of governmental functions. The report made by the county superintendent of Jefferson County, Florida, published in the *State Superintendent's Biennial Report* for 1898-1900 is indicative of that early opposition which still persists to some extent. In referring to concentration he wrote:

This is the keynote to any substantial improvement in county schools, but how it is to be accomplished in the face of the determined opposition

[3] *Bulletin No. 22, 1925,* United States Bureau of Education.

brought to bear by patrons and teachers on county boards and superintendents is a difficult problem. The demand is always for more schools with the inevitable result of dividing the school funds, by very long division, and multiplying low grade schools with short terms. Fewer and better schools should be the aim of every school officer.

Another Florida county superintendent in this same period stated:

I was born and reared a Democrat and as such am opposed to this pernicious movement of concentration.

The rural people of the United States live out on their farms for the most part and are not concentrated in villages as in Europe. This is partly a result of early homesteading laws which compelled actual residence on the land in order to establish the claim. This has tended to make the American farmer perhaps more individualistic than ordinary. Some sociologists believe that that is desirable, and others believe its dangers offset the benefits. Some who believe that it is better for every man to have his own kingdom and dwell in it fear that the concentration of schools will depopulate the farms. This feeling is seen in the following excerpt taken from the report of the state commissioner of Maine: [4]

There has been much prejudice on the part of the people in regard to the centralizing or consolidating of our schools. It has been claimed by some that this method is forcing the people to move out of the country places and is in a measure depopulating the country towns.

These apprehensions are due to fear of the excessive cost of concentration and transportation and to the belief that the newer type of education will "educate the boy away from the farm." It is feared that he will either leave the farm, or, if he does farm, he will live in town and operate it as a non-resident. It is argued that taking the school out of his community and centralizing the control will take his interest out of the local community and turn it toward the town which is most likely to be the center of the consolidation.

Some educators are inclined to view with alarm the mounting expenditure for transportation incumbent upon consolidation. In a letter addressed to the county superintendents of New Jersey by the State Department of Education in 1916, it was

[4] Report of the State Commissioner of Education of the State of Maine for the School Biennium ending June 30, 1926.

stated that it was desired that expenses for transportation should not increase any faster than was absolutely necessary. J. F. Abel,[5] assistant superintendent in rural education of the United States Bureau of Education, stated:

> Transportation is a comparatively new item in school budgets, and in some sections of the country there seems to be a tendency to give it too high a percentage of the funds. . . .

Transportation expenditures are looked upon as non-educational expenditures and as such should be curbed as much as possible. Some of this opposition has grown out of hasty and ill-advised consolidations.

Other educators insist that it has never been definitely established that a high type of educational offering is not possible in the one-room rural school, and are loath to discard it without objective proof of its inadequacy. Those advocating concentration admit that it might be possible to offer a high type of education in a one-room rural school, but insist that the cost of providing an educational opportunity equivalent to that of a centralized school in the one-room school is prohibitive. They point out that it is possible to employ better trained teachers, provide better equipment, and in effect provide an entire educational environment of a superior nature in a centralized school. It is a matter of common sense to assume a better educational output.

Then, too, the old sentiment for the "little red schoolhouse" has been a powerful factor in the opposition. That little school was the culmination of an ideal for which they had labored in the fight for public education. Some of them had helped to lay the foundation stones upon which it stands. They had donated their time and efforts freely for its erection. Perhaps their parents, their grandparents, or their great-grandparents, as well as they, had once gone to that school. When those of the newer generation insinuate that the little red school is an abomination, a very natural opposition is aroused.

Coupled with sentiment, but not so noble in nature, is man's universal love of domination and the exercise of authority. The board member of the little one-room schoolhouse has guided the educational destinies of the "district school" for generations. To relinquish that authority to some other man, who will probably

5 *Bulletin No. 32, 1924*, United States Bureau of Education.

be some man from the town which will most likely be the center of the consolidation, is distasteful to him, even though he knows that it will be for the educational betterment of his community. Quite frequently he believes that the people who live in town are, for a great part, social parasites, and that they already have too much authority in the community. His last stronghold is the district school, and he views with disfavor any attempt to wrest it from his control.

Despite all these interplaying forces, however, the idealism of the American farmer is winning out. He is not a peasant in any sense of the word. He does not believe that because he is a farmer his sons must be farmers or his daughters must be farmers' wives. He has faith in the ideals of American democracy, believing it possible that some day his own son might occupy the White House. Holding that faith, he wants an educational offering for his child equivalent to any in the land. Any attempt to institute a caste system of education in which his children cannot become bankers, lawyers, doctors, or enter any profession, occupation, or vocation arouses his most bitter opposition. He is realizing that if his children are educated in a community with a one-room rural school, taught by an incompetent teacher, with no high school facilities, that they will be unable to compete with their urban colleagues. So, at a time when the favorable margin between the farmers' buying and selling dollar is growing narrower and narrower, they are still voting consolidations by overwhelming majorities, they are transporting at their own expense and paying tuition of thousands of their children to other schools, and they are demanding accredited high schools which will give varied curricula and which will prepare them for entrance into the best colleges and universities in the nation.

All the transportation of school children in the United States is not being carried on in the rural schools. Thousands of physical defectives are being transported in our large cities. Large building units have necessitated some transportation of normal children even in cities. However, the bulk of school transportation is being carried on in rural areas.

Believing in a continuation of this movement which will cause the expenditure of increased millions of dollars for the transportation of hundreds of thousands of school children, the following chapters are devoted to a consideration of some of the problems involved in the acceptance of the transportation of pupils as a public responsibility.

CHAPTER II

DEFINITION OF THE PROBLEM

New Concept of Meaning of "Equality of Opportunity"

The principle of state responsibility for the provision of educational opportunities for its citizens is now universal in the United States. The degree to which the state should participate in and administer its educational program is still a matter of experiment. That the state is responsible for providing an equality of educational opportunity throughout its borders has become one of the fundamental principles of our democracy. By "equality" is not meant sameness or uniformity of educational offering, but that every child has the right to a type of opportunity suited to the development of his individual capacities to their fullest extent. To give this statement as a quotation from one man would be to cheapen it, for it is taken from the lips of thousands of forward-looking educational statesmen.

The state, once recognizing its responsibility, was next faced with the necessity of translating that concept into action. America is rather firmly committed to a scheme of democracy in which the local community is preserved as an entity. There is always that interplay and balancing of the proper function of the local and the total units in every type of governmental activity. It is not a question of whether a local unit should be in existence or not, but what that local unit is to be. In education, should the unit be the state, the county, the township, the parish, the town, the district, or some other geographical division? Then still more perplexing is the question—What should be the duties and responsibilities of each unit and sub-unit?

Just what the state's responsibility for education means is now shaping itself rapidly into a definite and objective obligation consistent with the underlying theories of our democracy. Mort [1] is the leader in this movement. He believed that state responsi-

[1] Mort, P. R., *The Measurement of Educational Need.*

8

bility was not a matter of theorizing and speculation but a problem capable of objective definition as a result of scientific research. Burns[2] has outlined this development in his study on *The Measurement of the Need for Transporting Pupils.* Under the influence of Strayer,[3] Mort made a radical departure in his proposal for the state's participation in its educational activities. He proposed the theory that all the taxpaying ability of the state should be equally burdened to provide a minimum educational offering for every child in the state. The program was to be administered largely by the local community, but the state was financially responsible for a minimum program in every community regardless of its effort. Effort was excluded as a basis of aid because the wealthiest communities were able to make the most effort and hence the whole principle of equalization was defeated. He then proceeded to measure that minimum program. The following criteria were set up as elements to be included in the minimum program:

1. An educational offering found in all the communities in the state when the equalization program takes effect should be included in the minimum program.

2. When, because of conditions over which the local community has little or no control, supplementary undertakings are necessary in order to make it possible to carry on any activity, chosen under the the first principle mentioned above, these undertakings should be included in the minimum program.

3. When additional offerings are required in order to supply educational returns commonly expected from the minimum program but which, because of conditions over which the local community has little or no control, may not be expected to materialize, these additional undertakings should be included in the minimum program.

4. If there is reason to believe that the inclusion of any element in a minimum program will have any other than a salutary effect upon the educational offering in any community or will bring about harm that is out of all proportion to the good involved in including it in the burden to be equalized, it should be omitted from the minimum program.[4]

Burns' Index for the Measurement of Transportation Needs

The transportation of pupils legitimately comes under the second of these criteria. Burns[5] developed an index for transportation needs which he suggested as a basis of the measurement

[2] Burns, R. L., *Measurement of the Need for Transporting Pupils.*
[3] Strayer, G. D. and Haig, R. M., *The Financing of Education in the State of New York*, p. 174.
[4] Mort, P. R., *State Support for Public Schools*, p. 8.
[5] Burns, R. L., *Measurement of the Need for Transporting Pupils.*

of the state's minimum program of transportation, and proposed a scheme for distributing aid for transportation on the basis of his index.

Burns developed his index by starting with the assumption that the state's minimum program of transportation might be taken as what the average community is doing with respect to its need. His next problem was to use some criterion of need for transportation which was beyond the control of the local community. Students of school transportation have recognized for some years that sparsely settled rural communities need to transport a larger per cent of their children than urban districts if they are to maintain centralized schools with equivalent opportunities. Following this lead, he made a careful study of the association of density of school population with the per cent of the average daily attendance transported in New Jersey counties and found it to be quite high. Believing that sparsely settled communities transported children longer distances on the average than dense communities, and that due to this the per pupil cost of transportation was higher in the sparsely settled communities, he sought a measure of the average distance children were transported in each county to introduce in his index as a weighting factor associated with cost. The measure he used was the square root of the quotient obtained by dividing the area of the county in square miles by the number of school buildings. His final measure of need was as follows:

$$\frac{\text{Pupils Transported}}{\text{A. D. A.}} \sqrt{\frac{\text{Area of County}}{\text{Number of School Buildings}}}$$

When he tested the association of this measure of need with density of school population, he found a curvilinear relationship existing but, by taking the log of the density, the association was rendered practically rectilinear. The independent variable by which he predicted the transportation need of the community was then the log of the quotient obtained by dividing the average daily attendance by the area. Burns used the function $Y = be^{aX}$ in which Y represents the transportation need and X the density of school population. This function expressed the relationship of the two variables. By taking the log of this function and finding that the association between the log of Y, the transportation load, and the log of X, the density of school population, was rectilinear, he determined the equation of the line [6] by the method of correlations and regressions and found it to be log $Y = 2.62 - .799\ X$. He then predicted the transportation need for each county, by merely substituting for X its value in terms of average daily attendance per square mile for each county. This need figure was in hypothetical units and had to be translated into dollars. This was done by dividing the transportation cost by the units of need, and he found the central tendency was about $20 per pupil. The units of need for each county were then multiplied by 20 and the resulting figure was the state's minimum program of transportation for each county in terms of dollars. Finally, he proposed that if a county was spending less than the minimum for transportation, the state should assume the entire cost of transportation in that county and that, in case a county was spending more than the minimum, the state would allow only the amount of the minimum in state aid, the local community making up the balance.

Burns' pioneer study was the point of departure in this study. Techniques presented and experiences gained in this research were of invaluable aid in further researches in this field which disclosed certain inadequacies in Burns' technique which could be remedied.

Limitations of That Index

The chief deficiencies of the method proposed by Burns for the state's participation in its transportation program are as follows:

1. An undiscovered relationship between cost variations and area per school building is used as a weighting factor in measuring transportation need which is out of proportion to actual cost variations independent of the control of the local community.

2. It does not provide the state with adequate administration controls over money distributed as aid for transportation.

These will be discussed in their order.

An examination of Table II in Burns' study [7] will show that the square root of the area divided by the number of buildings for Hudson County was .606 and for Ocean 3.285, a ratio of over five to one. The writer fitted regression lines to trans-

---

[6] Burns, R. L., *Measurement of the Need For Transporting Pupils*, p. 28.
[7] Burns, R. L., *Measurement of the Need for Transporting Pupils*, p. 21.

portation costs as related to density and found that the widest cost variations were about three to one. The use of density as the independent predictive variable for costs is justified later in this study. It is unsafe to use any weighting factor for cost whose influence is not known. This weighting factor, however, is not so far at fault except in individual cases as it would at first seem, because its association with density of school population is positive and, as will be shown later in this study, cost of transportation is closely associated with density.

The weighting factor for costs should be based on some independent variable beyond the control of the community. Further researches presented later show that it is possible to smooth out the unusual fluctuations of the cost weighting factor by using a predictive variable beyond the control of the community and smoothed weighting values taken from the equation of a line fitted to costs as related to the independent variable density of school population.

Burns' index does not furnish the state with adequate administrative controls for the distribution of state aid for transportation because the minimum program is given in hypothetical units and dollars only. According to this plan, if a county spends $75,000 or more, the state will allow all of the county's expenditures for transportation in its program for aid. It is quite possible that the community is providing a type of transportation which should not be included in the minimum. For instance, two counties, each with similar factors affecting cost, might be spending widely different amounts in effecting the same transportation due to variations in efficiency of local management. A county receiving $75,000 might be transporting only 1,000 children, when other counties with similar conditions are furnishing 2,000 children with adequate transportation for the same amount of money. Obviously, the state should not encourage inefficiency and extravagance in its program of support.

Statement of the Problem

A new measure of transportation need and method of administering state aid is presented in the next few chapters which, it is believed, remedy these deficiencies and provide the most advanced method yet proposed for the state's participation in its transportation program.

The latter part of this study is concerned with an analysis of local administrative problems and the development of a system of business management and cost accounting for the purpose of furthering efficient state and local administration of transportation.

CHAPTER III

DETERMINATION OF THE MINIMUM PROGRAM OF TRANSPORTATION IN TERMS OF PER CENT OF THE AVERAGE DAILY ATTENDANCE TRANSPORTED

Transportation has been frequently referred to as a non-educational expenditure. Strictly speaking, this is true. But the objective of the state is not necessarily the expenditure of the maximum percentage of its school funds for strictly educational expenditures but to bring to all its children the best educational offering possible per dollar of expenditure. Thus a community with a centralized school might be providing more educational opportunity for its children by spending 20 cents of every school dollar for transportation than a non-centralized community with one-room schools which is contributing nothing to the non-educational expenditure of transportation. The same can be said of all administrative and other expense coming under the general classification of overhead. The state, in providing the gigantic program of mass education being attempted in the "great American experiment in democracy" should, and is, recognizing these local adjustments. It is the problem of the succeeding pages to discover the need and propose the administration of one of these adjustments, namely, school transportation.

STANDARDS FOR A VALID MEASURE

In this development, these standards have been followed:

1. That the state should recognize the transportation being carried on in the average community in a group of communities whose needs for transportation are similar due to approximately equal effects of factors beyond the control of those communities, as the basis of the minimum program it will recognize in terms of numbers of students transported.

2. That the state should recognize as the per pupil cost of its minimum program the price paid by the average community in

a group of communities whose costs for transportation are affected similarly by factors beyond its control.

3. That the state should recognize in its program of support the transportation done within the minimum determined on the basis of (1) and at a cost within the legitimate minimum determined by (2).

4. That state aid for transportation should not be computed independent of the rest of the state's program of support, but should be combined with it and distributed on the basis of the community's ability to support education.

5. That the state in administering its program of support should not by its administration of those funds encourage local inefficiency or extravagance or render the community inflexible to educational change or reorganization as the science of education progresses.

6. That if it is shown in the administering of the plan that communities by reason of factors beyond their control have a transportation need at variance with that predicted by the selected independent variable, or variables, that variation should be included in the minimum program.

There is nothing startlingly new or unusual in these principles. In reading Mort's [1] *State Support for Public Schools,* one will be struck with a similarity that is in effect almost a rewording of some principles advanced in that work. Burns first presented (1) as a basis of determining the minimum program of transportation. Mort suggested (4) and (6) in *State Support for Public Schools.* The writer derived (2), (3), and (5) largely from the principles advanced by Mort and Burns. The major emphasis of this work is concerned with applying these principles administratively.

The first step is to measure a community's need for transportation in terms of pupils to be transported. This involves the use of a certain amount of statistical and mathematical techniques, but only those techniques are used which will throw light on the data in hand and assist in their intelligent interpretation. All the steps are presented to the end that they might be of assistance to someone working on a similar problem.

As Burns showed in New Jersey, and as is further shown in the following pages by evidence presented from four other states—

[1] Mort, P. R., *State Support for Public Schools.*

Pennsylvania, Connecticut, Alabama, and Florida—with widely different local conditions, there is a strong association between the per cent of the average daily attendance transported and the density of school population per square mile in the several school administrative units. Data from the state of Pennsylvania were studied first. Pennsylvania has a total area of 44,832 square miles of territory, 67 counties, and had an average daily attendance of 1,550,274 in the year 1926-1927, as is shown in Table 4. The average area of the counties is 669.1 square miles, and the average density is 28.91876 children in average daily attendance per square mile of territory. Forty-eight thousand one hundred ninety-four children were transported to school at public expense in this state in 1926-1927. The percentage of the average daily attendance transported varied from .1472 in York County to 26.2033 in Pike County.

Selection of Predictive Variable

The problem is to find the relationship that exists between the per cent of the average daily attendance transported and the density of school population, and express it objectively in terms of a mathematical relationship. This curved line of relationship, which it later proves to be, is best determined by first locating as definite and reliable points in the path of relationship as is possible. This is done by grouping the counties in intervals of seven in average daily attendance per square mile and calculating the average per cent transported for each group. The results of this procedure are reported in Table 2 and the number of counties in each density group reported opposite. Montgomery and Delaware Counties are excluded because of unusual departure from their density groups which would unduly weight the average. Philadelphia, Allegheny, and Lackawanna are averaged and grouped at a density of 120-126 because an examination of the data shows that there is no relation between density and per cent transported above this point, all counties of greater density having the tendency to transport equivalent percentages of their average daily attendance. The group averages are shown plotted on the broken line in Plate 4.

The next step is to write the equation of the smoothed curve that best fits the relationship existing between the two variables, per cent transported and density of school population. The problem is one of curve fitting and is not a process of blind trial and error in fitting one function after another to the data and testing its fit, but one of intelligent utilization of every known bit of evidence that will throw light on the data in hand. The Pearson coefficient of correlation is — .6398, but the variables are so obviously related curvilinearly to each other that this coefficient is useless because it assumes linearity. This r is reported without a probable error, for the formula for probable error assumes an equal chance of variation plus or minus, and, since the relationship is known to be non-linear,[2] the actual correlation is almost certainly higher than the computed value.

From this point, the actual per cent of the average daily attendance transported will be referred to as the Y, or ordinate value, and the average daily attendance per square mile as the density of school population, the X or the abscissa value. The predicted value of Y will be designated as $\tilde{Y}_p$.

This much is known about the properties of the variables whose relationship is sought and which must be included in the equation of their relationship.

1. They are related inversely to each other.

2. The predicted or $\tilde{Y}_p$ must have a finite value when $X = 0$ or else, as values of X approach 0, the $\tilde{Y}_p$ will be unreasonably large.

3. No value of $\tilde{Y}_p$ can ever be negative and thus all values of $\tilde{Y}_p$ must lie in the first quadrant of the coördinate axes for all rational values of X.

SELECTION OF THE FUNCTION

Other things being equal, the wisest thing to do is to select the simplest function possible to express this relationship. The function $Y = \dfrac{A}{X}$ satisfies the first requirement that the variables be related to each other inversely, but violates the second requirement in that Y is infinity if X equals 0, for this line is asymptotic to the Y axis as X approaches 0 and to the X axis as X approaches infinity. This curve satisfies the third condition, namely, that there should be no negative values of Y for rational values of X, for if the curve never approaches the X axis closer than the point of tangency, no negative values of Y are possible. The weakness

[2] Burns, R. L., *Measurement of the Need for Transporting Pupils*, p. 14.

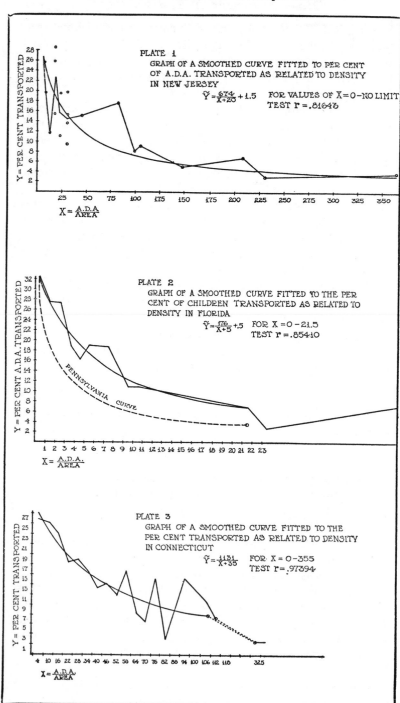

PLATE 1

GRAPH OF A SMOOTHED CURVE FITTED TO PER CENT OF A.D.A. TRANSPORTED AS RELATED TO DENSITY IN NEW JERSEY

$\hat{Y} = \frac{674}{X+20} + 1.5$ FOR VALUES OF X=0—NO LIMIT TEST r = .81643

Y = PER CENT TRANSPORTED

$X = \frac{A.D.A}{AREA}$

PLATE 2

GRAPH OF A SMOOTHED CURVE FITTED TO THE PER CENT OF CHILDREN TRANSPORTED AS RELATED TO DENSITY IN FLORIDA

$\hat{Y} = \frac{176}{X+5} + .5$ FOR X=0—21.5 TEST r = .85410

Y = PER CENT A.D.A. TRANSPORTED

PENNSYLVANIA CURVE

$X = \frac{A.D.A.}{AREA}$

PLATE 3

GRAPH OF A SMOOTHED CURVE FITTED TO THE PER CENT TRANSPORTED AS RELATED TO DENSITY IN CONNECTICUT

$\hat{Y} = \frac{1131}{X+35}$ FOR X=0—355 TEST r = .97394

Y = PER CENT TRANSPORTED

$X = \frac{A.D.A.}{AREA}$

PLATES 1, 2 AND 3

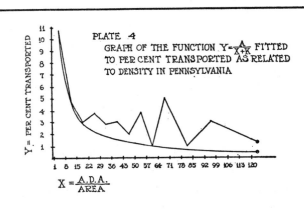

PLATE 4

GRAPH OF THE FUNCTION $Y = \frac{A}{X+K}$ FITTED TO PER CENT TRANSPORTED AS RELATED TO DENSITY IN PENNSYLVANIA

Y = PER CENT TRANSPORTED

$X = \frac{A.D.A.}{AREA}$

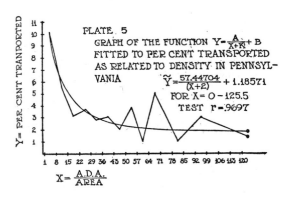

PLATE 5

GRAPH OF THE FUNCTION $Y = \frac{A}{X+K} + B$ FITTED TO PER CENT TRANSPORTED AS RELATED TO DENSITY IN PENNSYLVANIA

$$\widetilde{Y} = \frac{57.44704}{(X+2)} + 1.18571$$

FOR $X = 0 - 125.5$

TEST $r = .9697$

Y = PER CENT TRANSPORTED

$X = \frac{A.D.A.}{AREA}$

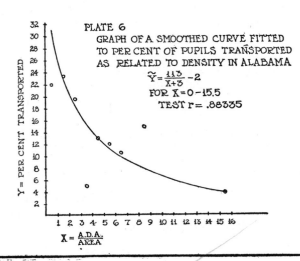

PLATE 6

GRAPH OF A SMOOTHED CURVE FITTED TO PER CENT OF PUPILS TRANSPORTED AS RELATED TO DENSITY IN ALABAMA

$$\widetilde{Y} = \frac{113}{X+3} - 2$$

FOR $X = 0 - 15.5$

TEST $r = .88335$

Y = PER CENT TRANSPORTED

$X = \frac{A.D.A.}{AREA}$

PLATES 4, 5, AND 6

of the function with respect to the second condition can easily be remedied by merely making the line tangent to a point in the second quadrant of the coördinate axes. This is accomplished by merely adding some positive quantity to the X value. What this value should be is a matter of experiment but, for the time being, the function can be written as $Y = \dfrac{A}{X + K}$.

Fitting of the Curve and Computation of the Constants

The problem now is to fit this function to the data and see what happens. This is conveniently done by the method of "least squares" if some arbitrary value as, for instance, 1, is assigned to K.[3] The theory of this method is simply that the line fits best when the sum of the squares of the deviations of the actual values from the predicted values is a minimum or the least possible. The complete steps in this process will be shown presently in the derivation of the final formula. The function as developed thus far was fitted to the data and is shown plotted in Plate 4. A study of the graph will show that the predicted values from the point of $X = 18.5 +$ are considerably lower than the actual values. The first thought that occurs is to lift this equation by merely adding a constant. But since the values of Y from $X = 0$ to 18.5 are already large enough, they would be increased too much by the addition of the constant. This can be remedied by making the line tangent to a point farther over in the second quadrant. This will shift the whole curve to the reader's left and consequently reduce the Y values between the values of $X = 0$ to 18.5 proportionately more than above 18.5. One is not entirely reduced to the process of trial and error in determining at just what point in the second quadrant the line should be made tangent. This value can be approximated by fitting a flexible ruler to the data in a curve of the approximate bend of the function being used. The ruler will be tangent to the approximate point desired. This value was determined to be 2. The function as now developed is $Y = \dfrac{A}{X + 2} + B$ and it can be fitted to the data by the method of least squares. Readers who are not interested in the mathematical calculation can omit this development with-

[3] Holzinger, Karl J., *Statistical Methods for Students in Education*, p. 320.

out losing the meaning of the chapter. The process is one of calculating the values of the constants A and B and is as given in the following:

1. Since Y is the actual value and $\frac{A}{X+2} + B$ is the predicted value, if their difference is found, squared, summed, and made a minimum as $\Sigma\left(Y - \left(\frac{A}{X+2} + B\right)\right)^2 =$ a minimum, the conditions of best fit will be satisfied.

2. Differentiating the function with respect to A by dividing through by its coefficient:

(a) $\Sigma f\left(\frac{Y}{X+2}\right) = A\Sigma\left(\frac{f}{(X+2)^2}\right) + B\Sigma\left(\frac{f}{(X+2)}\right)$ where $f =$ frequency.

3. Differentiating with respect to B by dividing through by its coefficient:

(b) $\Sigma fY = A\Sigma\left(\frac{f}{X+2}\right) + NB.$

4. The equations (a) and (b) are simultaneous equations in two unknowns, A and B, for the other values f, Y, and X are known, being the original data themselves. The calculation of their actual values is shown in Table 2. They are then substituted in equations (a) and (b) which can then readily be solved by substitution. The value of A is found to be 57.44704, and that of B to be 1.18571. Substituting these values in the original function, the final equation of the line of relationship existing between the density of school population and the per cent transported is $\tilde{Y}_p = \dfrac{57.44704}{X+2}$ $+\ 1.18571$. It is a simple matter to substitute for X its value and to solve the equation for $\tilde{Y}_p$. The line is shown plotted in Plate 5.

5. To the eye it looks at once like a good fit, but it must be remembered that the departures of the broken line have different weights because of different numbers of frequencies at their location. For instance, the wide fluctuation of the broken line at $X = 67.5$ has little significance, because there is only one county in that group. If the predicted value of the first step, where $X = 4.5$, had been off the broken line very far, it would have been serious because the frequency of that group is 16. A good

measure of the fit of a line is that used by Burns[4] which he derived from Yule.[5] It is as follows:

$$r = \sqrt{1 - \frac{\Sigma(Y - \tilde{Y})^2}{N \sqrt{\sigma Y^2}}}$$

It is known as the generalized coefficient of correlation. An examination of this formula shows that it is based on the accuracy of the predictive power of the equation. If the curve fitted perfectly, there would be no departure and hence the maximum value of r is 1. The minimum value of r approaches 0 and then passes to an imaginary number. The fit of this line is found to be .9697. In order to approach this high value, two things are necessary. First, the line must be a good fit to the data, and second, the variables must really have a high association. No matter how good the fit, it would not show a high test unless there was a symmetrical relationship running through the data. Thus, the limiting factor of a good fit is the degree of association between the variables. The inference of this reasoning is that the equation $\tilde{Y}_p = \frac{57.44704}{X + 2} + 1.18571$ is a valid measure of the per cent of the average daily attendance transported to be included in the state's minimum program because the function is a good fit and there is a high association between the per cent of the average daily attendance transported and the density of school population which is used as the predictive variable.

The application of this equation to Pennsylvania counties is shown in Table 4. The predicted per cent of the average daily attendance to be transported within the minimum program is designated by $\tilde{Y}_p$.

Other functions, some quite complicated, were tested to ascertain if a better fit could be obtained,[6] but none was found. The exponential function Burns used, $Y = be^{aX}$, could be used with fair results, but it is a complicated function difficult to fit to data. If the log of the density of school population happens to relate itself to the log of the per cent transported in a rectilinear fashion, then the fitting is relatively simple but this cannot be assured in every state.

[4] Burns, R. L., *Measurement of the Need for Transporting Pupils*, p. 30.
[5] Yule, U. G., *An Introduction to the Theory of Statistics*, p. 204.
[6] Elderton, W. P., *Frequency Curves and Correlations*, p. 46.

TABLE 2

The Constants Are Calculated by the Method of Least Squares for the Function $Y = \dfrac{A}{X+2} + B$ When Fitted to the Group Average Per Cent Transported (Y Values) Picked Out by Density in Intervals of 7 (X Values)
(Data from Pennsylvania)

X Density	Y_p Average Per Cent Transported	f Frequency	$(X+2)$	$\dfrac{f}{(X+2)}$	$(X+2)^2$	$\dfrac{f}{(X+2)^2}$	fY_p	$\dfrac{Y_p}{(X+2)}$	$\dfrac{Y_p}{(X+2)}$	$\hat{Y}_p$	$Y_p - \hat{Y}_p$	$(Y_p - \hat{Y}_p)^2$	$(Y_p - \hat{Y}_p)^2$
1– 7	10.25	16	6.5	2.46154	42.25	.37870	164.00	1.57692	25.23072	10.02371	.226	.051	.816
8– 14	5.00	12	13.5	.88889	182.25	.06584	60.00	.37037	4.44444	5.44104	−.441	.194	2.328
15– 21	3.2	10	20.5	.48780	420.25	.02380	32.00	.15610	1.56100	3.98801	−.788	.621	6.210
22– 28	3.67	6	27.5	.21818	756.25	.00793	22.02	.13345	.80070	3.27469	.395	.156	.936
29– 35	2.75	4	34.5	.11594	1190.25	.00336	11.00	.07971	.31884	2.85084	−.101	.010	.040
36– 42	3.0	1	41.5	.02410	1722.25	.00058	3.00	.07229	.07229	2.56998	.430	.185	.185
43– 49	2.0	2	48.5	.04124	2352.25	.00085	4.00	.04124	.08248	2.37019	−.370	.137	.274
50– 56	3.67	6	55.5	.10811	3080.25	.00195	22.02	.06613	.39678	2.21079	1.459	2.129	12.774
57– 63	1.0	2	62.5	.03200	3906.25	.00051	2.00	.01600	.03200	2.10486	−1.105	1.221	2.442
64– 70	5.0	1	69.5	.01439	4380.25	.00023	5.00	.07194	.07194	2.01229	2.988	8.928	8.928
78– 84	1.0	1	83.5	.01198	6982.25	.00014	3.00	.01198	.01198	1.87370	−.874	.764	.764
92– 98	3.0	1	97.5	.01026	9506.25	.00011	3.00	.03077	.03077	1.77491	1.225	1.501	1.501
120–126	1.33	3	125.5	.02390	15750.25	.00019	3.00	.00797	.02391	1.63344	−.306	.094	.282
Total		35		4.43833	.	.48419	332.04		33.07785				37.480

SUMMARY

1. The problem of the chapter was to determine the relationship existing between some independent variable and the per cent of the average daily attendance transported to be included in the state's minimum program.

2. A set of standards were set up as criteria of the validity of the procedure.

3. The independent predictive variable selected was average daily attendance per square mile.

4. The determined relationship $\hat{Y}_p = \dfrac{57.44704}{X + 2} + 1.18571$ is a valid predictive index of the number of children to be transported because the function fits the data well and a high association exists between density of school population and per cent of average daily attendance transported.

CHAPTER IV

DETERMINATION OF THE COST PER PUPIL TRANSPORTED DUE TO FACTORS BEYOND THE CONTROL OF THE LOCAL COMMUNITY

SELECTION OF PREDICTIVE VARIABLE

It is a well-known fact that some school boards must pay more to transport their children than others, due to factors beyond their control. Of these factors, the principal ones are availability of public service lines for the use of schools, type of roads, length of haul, scatter of children, cost of living, and competition between transportation contractors. Happily, these factors are all associated, some positively and some negatively, with density of population. The hypothesis assumed, which is later tested, is that density of population, being itself associated with the principal factors affecting cost, could be considered as a summation of the effects of these various factors on cost, some positive and some negative, and thus used as an independent variable predicting cost.

SELECTION OF FUNCTIONS FOR EXPRESSION OF EXISTING RELATIONSHIP

The same method of attack was used as in Chapter III, the average cost per pupil transported being calculated for density group intervals of 7. The data are given in Table 3. They are shown plotted in Plate 9. The eye is at once caught with the regularity of their arrangement. The Pearson r of density of school population with group average cost per pupil, allowing each average its frequency weight, is —.99279 for 61 of the 67 Pennsylvania counties ranging in density from 1 to 84. The probable error of this r is ±.00124 if the N is considered the number of counties concentrated at the group average. If the N is considered the number of group averages, the probable error is still only ±.00280. The coefficient of correlation —.99279

25

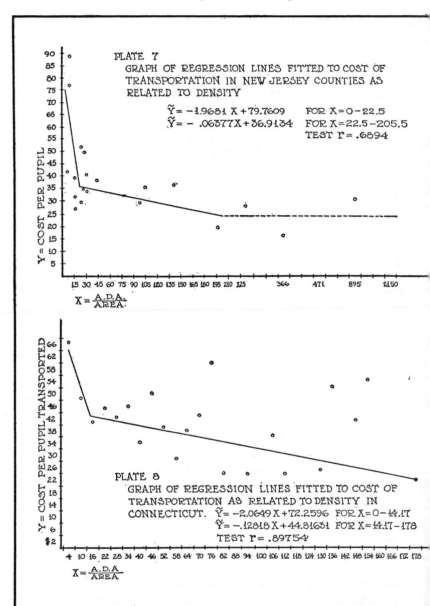

PLATE 7
GRAPH OF REGRESSION LINES FITTED TO COST OF
TRANSPORTATION IN NEW JERSEY COUNTIES AS
RELATED TO DENSITY

$$\tilde{Y} = -1.9681\,X + 79.7609 \quad \text{FOR } X = 0-22.5$$
$$\tilde{Y} = -.06377\,X + 36.9134 \quad \text{FOR } X = 22.5-205.5$$
$$\text{TEST } r = .6894$$

$$X = \frac{A.D.A.}{AREA}$$

PLATE 8
GRAPH OF REGRESSION LINES FITTED TO COST OF
TRANSPORTATION AS RELATED TO DENSITY IN
CONNECTICUT. $\tilde{Y} = -2.0649\,X + 72.2596$ FOR $X = 0-14.17$
$\tilde{Y} = -.12818\,X + 44.81631$ FOR $X = 14.17-178$
TEST $r = .89754$

$$X = \frac{A.D.A}{AREA}$$

PLATES 7 AND 8

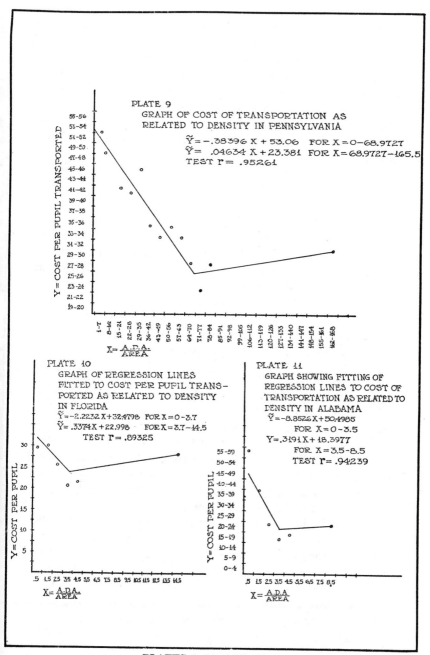

PLATE 9

GRAPH OF COST OF TRANSPORTATION AS RELATED TO DENSITY IN PENNSYLVANIA

$\tilde{Y} = -.38396 X + 53.06$ FOR $X = 0-68.9727$
$\tilde{Y} = .04634 X + 23.381$ FOR $X = 68.9727-165.5$
TEST $r = .95261$

$Y = $ COST PER PUPIL TRANSPORTED

$X = \dfrac{A.D.A.}{AREA}$

PLATE 10

GRAPH OF REGRESSION LINES FITTED TO COST PER PUPIL TRANSPORTED AS RELATED TO DENSITY IN FLORIDA

$\tilde{Y} = -2.2232 X + 32.4798$ FOR $X = 0-3.7$
$\tilde{Y} = .3374 X + 22.998$ FOR $X = 3.7-14.5$
TEST $r = .89325$

$Y = $ COST PER PUPIL

$X = \dfrac{A.D.A.}{AREA}$

PLATE 11

GRAPH SHOWING FITTING OF REGRESSION LINES TO COST OF TRANSPORTATION AS RELATED TO DENSITY IN ALABAMA

$\tilde{Y} = -8.8526 X + 50.4985$
FOR $X = 0-3.5$
$Y = .3191 X + 18.3977$
FOR $X = 3.5-8.5$
TEST $r = .94239$

$Y = $ COST PER PUPIL

$X = \dfrac{A.D.A.}{AREA}$

PLATES 9, 10, AND 11

is therefore remarkably high and indicative of rectilinear association within the range of the densities correlated. Cities
beyond the density of 84 tended to pay slightly more per pupil
up to a density of 165.5. Beyond that point, there seemed to be
no trend. The scarcity of cases at this point in the scale was a
handicap. The costs per pupil for those counties of high density
were averaged and grouped at the density point 165.5. Two
counties were omitted from the density group averages because
of unusual fluctuations which would unduly weight the group
average.

The problem now is to discover the equation of relationship
of density to cost. It will be observed in Plate 9 that the
cost per pupil appears to relate itself to density in a straight
line until a density of 85 is reached, and then it appears to rise
slightly. The same conditions as to fit stated in Chapter III
apply in this chapter. Due to the fact that the relationship was
so decidedly linear below a density of 84 including 61 counties,
it was decided to use two regression lines to describe the relationship, one for values of $X = 0$ to 68.9727, and the other for values
of $X = 68.9727 - 165.5$. The method of fitting these lines was
by the simple technique of correlations and regressions which
require no explanation to the reader.

Writing of Cost Equations

The symbol $\breve{Y}_c$ will be used to designate the predicted cost in
this chapter, and X will be density, as before. The regression
equation for values of $X = 0 - 68.9727$ is: (a) $\breve{Y}_c = - .38396$
$X + 53.060$. For values of $X = 68.9727 - 165.5$, (b) $\breve{Y}_c = .04634$
$X + 23.381$. All values of X greater than 165.5 will be considered
as equivalent to 165.5 and the Y for that value will be used. These
lines within their defined limits satisfy the conditions laid down
in Chapter III which also apply here.

The standard error of estimate for equation (a) is ± 1.058.
This equation contains the great majority of the counties. The
standard error of estimate for equation (b) is not reported because it contains so few cases that its constants were calculated
by merely sloping a line to the average of the costs of the
counties above a density of 165.5 from the average cost of the
groups surrounding the point where the two lines intersect.

The next task is to test the fit of these lines. This was done

ih the same manner as in Chapter III and was found to be
$r = .95261$. This is about as high a test as could be expected.
As was pointed out in Chapter III, a perfect fit would not be
desirable, for much of the fluctuation between these group averages is due to an insufficient number of cases in each step. The
technique of curved and straight line fitting takes care of this de-
ficiency admirably, for the unusual fluctuation of the average of
one interval is pulled back to normalcy by the influence of the

TABLE 3

COMPUTATION OF REGRESSION EQUATIONS FOR COST OF TRANSPORTATION AS
RELATED TO DENSITY IN PENNSYLVANIA

X Density	f Counties	Y_c Cost per Pupil	$\tilde{Y}_c$ Cost per Pupil
4.5	16	53.07	51.32
11.5	12	49.09	48.64
18.5	10	42.50	45.96
25.5	6	41.83	43.27
32.5	4	46.00	40.58
39.5	1	35.50	37.89
46.5	2	33.50	35.21
53.5	6	35.17	32.52
60.5	1	33.50	29.83
67.5	1	28.50	27.14
74.5	1	23.50	26.83
81.5	1	28.50	27.16
165.5	4	31.05	31.05

surrounding intervals. Thus a value secured from a fitted line or
curve is a sort of horizontal average for all values of the
dependent variable. In some statistical work this is not desired,
and the worth of the regression values is measured largely by its
ability to predict individual values. Happily, the opposite is
desired in this situation, for the regression equations or the curvilinear function developed in the preceding chapter would be
undesirable if they were sensitive to individual fluctuations.
What the state desires to discover is that general trend as indicated by the averages of the experiences of the several counties,
each considered as an unweighted experiment in school transportation.

The application of these equations to predicted costs for Pennsylvania counties is shown in Table 4, the predicted costs being designated as $\breve{Y}_c$.

SUMMARY

1. The density of school population is a valid, independent variable for the prediction of per pupil costs of transportation because the two variables are highly associated.

2. The relationship existing between the two variables can be expressed by two regression lines fulfilling the conditions necessary for a successful fit.

3. The equations $\breve{Y}_c = -.38396\,X + 53.06$ for values of $X = 0$ —68.9727 and $\breve{Y}_c = .04634\,X + 23.381$ for values of $X = 68.9727$ —165.5 for the state of Pennsylvania for the test of fit is high and a strong association exists between the independent predictive variable and the variable whose prediction is desired.

CHAPTER V

APPLICATION OF THE INDICES TO THE ADMINISTRA-
TION OF STATE AID FOR TRANSPORTATION IN
PENNSYLVANIA

Computation of Transportation Need in Terms of Per Cent of Average Daily Attendance Transported

The final step is to apply these indices to the distribution of state aid for transportation. The steps in this process are relatively simple, two of which have already been taken.

1. Determine the per cent of the children to be transported in each county within the state's minimum program by substituting its density of school population as measured by average daily attendance per square mile for X in the equation $\breve{Y}_p = \dfrac{57.44707}{X+2} + 1.18571$.

2. Multiply the average daily attendance by $\breve{Y}_p$ and the result is the number of students to be transported within the state's minimum program.

3. If the county is transporting a number equal to or greater than this minimum, allow only the number in the minimum. If a county is transporting less than the minimum, allow only the number transported.

4. Determine the cost per pupil transported by substituting the density of the school population for X in the equation $\breve{Y}_c = -.38396\ X + 53.06$ if $X = 0$—68.9727 or the equation $\breve{Y}_c = .04634\ X + 23.381$ if $X = 68.9727$—165.5. Consider all values of X higher than 165.5 as 165.5 and substitute in the equation accordingly.

5. Multiply the number of students transported for whom aid is allowed by $\breve{Y}_c$. The result is the calculated value of what the transportation of the pupils for whom aid is allowed should cost in that county.

6. If the actual reported cost for all transportation is less than the calculated cost of the transportation for which the county is

allowed state aid, allow only the amount the county is spending. If the county is spending an amount for transportation equal to or above the calculated cost of the transportation they are doing for which aid is allowed, the calculated cost is the total aid allowed that county.

These calculations are made for all counties in Pennsylvania in Table 4. Perhaps it will be of value to the reader to take two counties as types and carry the calculations through.

The data for Adams County are: Average daily attendance—5,683; density—10.7633; number transported—101; total cost—$4,523.

1. Substitute the density 10.7633 in the equation

$$\tilde{Y} = \frac{57.44707}{X + 2} + 1.18571$$
$$= \frac{57.44707}{10.7633 + 2} + 1.18571$$
$$= 5.68667$$

2. Multiply $5,683 \times 5.68667 = 323$ which is the minimum program in terms of numbers transported for this county.

3. Adams County transported only 101 students so that is the number transported for which the state will allow aid.

4. Substitute the density 10.7633 in the equation

$$\tilde{Y}_c = -.38396X + 53.06$$
$$= -.38396 \times 10.7633 + 53.06$$
$$= \$48.93$$

5. Multiply $101 \times \$48.93 = \$4,941.93$ which is the calculated cost for transportation in Adams County for which aid is allowed.

6. But the actual cost of transportation in Adams County is only $4,523 so that is the amount of aid it will be allowed.

The data for Cambria County are: Average daily attendance—40,317; density—56.2301; number transported—880; total cost—$33,753.

1. Substitute the density 56.2301 for X in the equation

$$\tilde{Y}_p = \frac{57.44707}{X + 2} + 1.18571$$
$$= \frac{57.44707}{56.2301 + 2} + 1.18571$$
$$= 2.17226$$

2. Multiply 40,317 × 2.17226 = 876 which is the minimum program in terms of numbers transported.

3. Cambria County transported 880 students so aid will be allowed for the minimum program only, which is 876.

4. Substitute the density 56.2301 for X in the equation

$$\tilde{Y}_c = - .38396 \, X + 53.06$$
$$= - .38396 \times 56.2301$$
$$= \$31.47$$

5. Multiply 876 × \$31.47 = \$27,567.72, which is the calculated cost of its transportation for which aid is allowed.

6. Cambria's actual cost was \$33,753, so the aid will be the calculated cost \$27,567.72.

Maximum Cost of Minimum Program

Table 4 is further developed for additional information that is of interest to the state department. If the total minimum program of each county in terms of numbers to be transported is multiplied by the $\tilde{Y}_c$ cost figure for that county and summed for the whole state, the resulting figure will be the outside cost of the minimum program of transportation in the state if every county transported up to the minimum. This will hardly happen, however. The maximum cost of the minimum program for transportation in Pennsylvania for 1926–1927 to be used as the basis for apportioning aid in 1928 is \$1,656,374.98. The actual aid to be apportioned for transportation in 1928 is \$1,163,665.

Combination of Transportation Need with Other Elements of Educational Need

As was stated earlier in this study, it is not an ideal plan for the state to carry on its program of state support by giving special aid to different projects irrespective of each other. Mort [1] is especially emphatic about this point. For the state to effect a program of equalization, aid must be distributed according to the community's ability to support education. It is, therefore, proposed that the proposed state aid for each county be lumped with the other elements of the minimum program for the several counties and distributed on the basis of the taxpaying abilities of the communities. The scheme proposed in this study blends admirably with the technique devised by Mort [2] by which the

---

[1] Mort, P. R., *State Support for Public Schools.*
[2] Mort, P. R., *The Measurement of Educational Need.*

APPLICATION OF THE FORMULAE TO THE DISTRIBUTION OF

County	Density A. D. A. Area	$\tilde{Y}_p{}^a$ Per Cent Transported	A. D. A.	Minimum Program in Terms of Pupils to be Transported	$\tilde{Y}_c{}^b$ Cost per Pupil Transported	Maximum Cost of Minimum Program if All Counties Transported Up to Minimum
Adams	10.7633	5.68667	5,683	323	$48.93	$15,804.39
Allegheny	270.9820	1.64346	196,462	3,229	31.05	100,260.45
Armstrong	23.9509	3.39939	15,640	532	43.86	23,333.52
Beaver	58.0489	2.14238	24,903	534	30.77	16,431.18
Bedford	7.9327	6.96934	8,139	567	50.01	28,355.67
Berks	38.9190	2.58963	33,665	872	38.12	33,240.64
Blair	45.5813	2.39305	24,386	583	35.56	20,731.48
Bradford	8.2160	6.80895	9,408	641	49.91	31,992.31
Bucks	25.1069	3.30499	15,265	505	43.42	21,927.10
Butler	20.6113	3.72634	16,283	607	45.15	27,406.05
Cambria	56.2301	2.17226	40,317	876	31.47	27,567.72
Cameron	2.8954	12.92061	1,135	147	51.96	7,638.12
Carbon	28.4458	3.07257	11,549	355	42.14	14,959.70
Centre	7.8307	7.02935	8,974	631	50.05	31,581.55
Chester	26.0837	3.23128	20,267	655	43.04	28,191.20
Clarion	11.4659	5.45182	6,891	376	48.66	18,296.16
Clearfield	19.0271	3.91776	21,729	851	45.75	38,933.25
Clinton	6.9169	7.62820	6,073	463	50.40	23,335.20
Columbia	20.9958	3.68386	10,057	370	45.00	16,650.00
Crawford	10.4750	5.79068	10,873	630	49.04	30,895.20
Cumberland	21.5568	3.62437	11,382	413	44.78	18,494.14
Dauphin	51.0307	2.26899	26,638	604	33.47	20,215.88
Delaware	167.1081	1.64346	30,915	508	31.05	15,773.40
Elk	7.4441	7.26856	6,000	436	50.20	21,887.20
Erie	32.9398	2.82988	25,726	728	40.41	29,418.48
Fayette	54.9484	2.19447	43,739	960	31.96	30,681.60
Forest	2.7028	13.40121	1,146	154	52.02	8,011.08
Franklin	16.3422	4.31767	12,273	530	46.79	24,798.70
Fulton	4.3697	10.20451	1,761	180	51.38	9,248.30
Greene	12.9930	5.01730	7,458	374	48.07	17,978.18
Huntington	8.2658	6.78167	7,588	515	49.89	25,693.35
Indiana	22.2027	3.55929	18,406	655	44.54	29,173.70
Jefferson	19.3559	3.87569	12,891	500	45.63	22,815.00
Juniata	7.0816	7.51136	2,776	209	50.34	10,521.06
Lackawanna	126.9579	1.64346	57,258	941	31.05	29,218.05
Lancaster	32.3210	2.85953	30,415	870	40.65	35,365.50
Lawrence	56.8861	2.16127	20,479	443	31.22	13,830.46
Lebanon	30.0750	2.97673	10,827	322	41.51	13,366.22
Lehigh	69.4478	1.98975	23,890	475	26.60	12,635.00
Luzerne	93.9283	1.78456	83,784	1,495	27.73	41,456.35
Lycoming	12.0450	5.27592	14,695	775	48.44	37,541.00
McKean	9.2087	6.31093	9,089	574	49.52	28,424.48
Mercer	27.6586	3.12265	19,361	605	42.44	25,676.20
Mifflin	17.9925	4.05914	7,161	291	46.15	13,429.65
Monroe	7.5490	7.20174	4,703	339	50.16	17,004.24
Montgomery	72.9793	1.95188	35,322	689	26.76	18,437.64
Montom	15.4615	4.47564	2,010	90	47.12	4,240.80
Northampton	83.2392	1.87585	30,965	581	27.24	15,826.44
Northumberland	48.2159	2.32971	21,890	510	34.55	17,620.50
Perry	8.1631	6.83822	4,604	315	49.93	15,727.95
Philadelphia	1,797.5234	1.64346	230,083	3,781	31.05	117,400.05
Pike	1.7188	16.63345	935	156	52.40	8,174.40
Potter	3.2260	12.17825	3,455	421	51.82	21,816.22
Schuylkill	55.1750	2.19047	42,871	939	31.88	29,935.32
Snyder	10.8778	5.64665	3,383	191	48.88	9,336.08
Somerset	18.6731	3.96454	19,303	765	45.89	35,105.85
Sullivan	3.9170	10.89452	1,794	195	51.56	10,054.20
Susquehanna	7.3835	7.29718	6,084	444	50.23	22,302.12
Tioga	5.6235	8.72123	6,422	560	50.90	28,504.00
Union	9.3082	6.26024	2,839	178	49.49	8,809.22
Venango	16.0257	4.37266	10,593	463	46.91	21,719.33
Warren	8.5865	6.61215	7,745	512	49.76	25,477.12
Washington	53.1751	2.22689	45,837	1,021	32.64	33,325.44
Wayne	6.8904	7.64740	5,092	389	50.41	19,609.49
Westmoreland	59.3109	2.12269	61,624	1,308	30.29	39,619.32
Wyoming	7.2796	7.37639	2,890	213	50.26	10,705.38
York	29.3167	3.02010	26,473	800	41.80	33,440.00
STATE	28.91876		1,550,274	42,164		1,656,374.98

* Data furnished by the State Department of Education for the school year 1926–1927.
ᵃ =Equation value of per cent to be transported in the minimum program.

STATE AID FOR TRANSPORTATION IN PENNSYLVANIA (1928)*

Actual Number Transported	Number of Students for Whom State Aid is Allowed 1926–27	Calculated Cost of Transportation Within Minimum Program	Proposed State Aid in Terms of Weighted Pupils	Y_p Actual Per Cent Transported	Y_c Actual Cost per Pupil	Actual Cost of Transportation	Proposed State Aid	Area in Square Miles
101	101	$4,941.93	96	1.7772	$44.78	$4,523	$4,523	528
3,076	3,076	95,509.80	2,037	1.5657	33.75	103,805	95,510	725
116	116	5,087.76	108	.7417	43.75	5,075	5,075	653
75	75	2,307.75	49	.3010	80.32	6,024	2,308	429
319	319	15,953.19	316	3.9195	46.40	14,802	14,802	1,026
908	872	33,240.64	659	2.6982	34.02	30,887	30,887	865
189	189	6,720.84	115	.7751	28.59	5,403	5,403	535
1,238	641	31,992.31	683	13.1591	54.35	67,286	31,992	1,145
1,049	505	21,927.10	468	6.8724	28.14	29,515	21,927	603
158	158	7,133.70	143	.9704	42.46	6,709	6,709	790
880	876	27,567.72	588	2.1828	38.36	33,753	27,568	717
95	95	4,936.20	105	8.3701	58.85	5,591	4,936	392
138	138	5,815.32	124	1.1950	42.80	5,907	5,815	406
357	357	17,867.85	333	3.9782	43.64	15,578	15,578	1,146
2,095	655	28,191.20	602	10.3371	26.03	54,537	28,191	777
388	376	18,672.16	355	5.6306	42.87	16,633	16,633	601
202	202	9,241.50	197	.9297	64.86	13,101	9,242	1,142
162	162	8,164.80	174	2.6676	56.09	9,087	8,165	878
422	370	16,650.00	315	4.1961	34.97	14,759	14,759	479
1,483	630	30,895.20	659	13.6393	42.54	63,085	30,895	1,038
370	370	16,568.60	152	3.2508	19.24	7,120	7,120	528
863	604	20,215.88	368	3.2398	19.97	17,233	17,233	522
2,135	508	15,773.40	336	6.9061	19.64	41,928	15,773	185
436	436	21,887.20	414	7.2667	44.52	19,411	19,411	806
1,088	728	29,418.48	628	4.2292	27.52	29,938	29,418	781
1,171	960	30,681.60	654	2.6773	73.34	85,877	30,682	796
93	93	4,837.86	103	8.1152	73.44	6,830	4,838	424
1,194	530	24,798.70	529	9.7287	30.04	35,864	24,799	751
55	55	2,825.90	60	3.1233	68.91	3,790	2,826	403
227	227	10,911.89	233	3.0438	81.25	18,443	10,912	574
255	255	12,721.95	190	3.3606	94.94	8,910	8,910	918
236	236	10,511.44	224	1.2822	47.43	11,194	10,511	829
125	125	5,703.75	122	.9697	48.03	6,004	5,704	666
173	173	8,708.82	95	6.2320	25.86	4,473	4,473	392
662	662	20,555.10	438	1.1562	37.05	24,580	20,555	451
773	773	31,422.45	670	2.5416	45.37	35,071	31,422	941
837	443	13,830.46	295	4.0872	18.41	15,407	13,830	360
358	322	13,366.22	285	3.2881	38.35	13,654	13,366	360
1,257	475	12,635.00	270	5.2617	28.90	36,332	12,635	344
1,811	1,495	41,456.35	884	2.1616	33.75	61,115	41,456	892
225	225	10,899.00	232	1.5312	64.88	14,598	10,899	1,220
297	297	14,707.44	314	3.2677	65.18	19,358	14,707	987
288	288	12,222.72	261	1.4876	60.97	17,558	12,223	700
166	166	7,660.90	105	2.3182	29.77	4,942	4,942	398
468	339	17,004.24	363	9.9511	37.19	17,403	17,004	623
4,686	689	18,437.64	393	13.2666	24.85	116,455	18,438	484
51	51	2,403.12	51	2.5374	57.98	2,957	2,403	130
116	116	3,159.84	67	.3749	28.65	3,323	3,160	372
775	510	17,620.50	376	3.5405	36.02	27,917	17,621	454
117	117	5,841.81	125	2.5413	52.68	6,163	5,842	564
2,900	2,900	90,045.00	1,921	1.2605	36.86	106,904	90,045	128
245	156	8,174.40	174	26.2033	73.24	17,944	8,174	544
375	375	19,432.50	415	10.8539	58.35	21,882	19,433	1,071
2,558	939	29,935.32	639	5.9668	31.41	80,340	29,935	777
60	60	2,932.80	49	1.7736	37.98	2,279	2,279	311
143	143	6,562.27	140	.7409	53.94	7,714	6,562	1,034
72	72	3,712.32	79	4.0134	79.07	5,693	3,712	458
1,041	444	22,302.12	476	17.1105	47.02	48,943	22,302	824
1,172	560	28,504.00	608	18.2498	48.42	56,752	28,504	1,142
138	138	6,829.62	41	4.8609	27.38	3,778	3,778	305
553	463	21,719.33	463	5.2205	47.51	26,273	21,719	661
768	512	25,477.12	543	9.9161	41.69	32,016	25,477	902
1,485	1,021	33,325.44	711	3.2398	28.64	42,525	33,325	862
555	389	19,609.49	418	10.8995	47.60	26,418	19,609	739
741	741	22,444.89	479	1.2025	33.11	24,535	22,445	1,039
592	213	10,705.38	228	20.4845	37.67	22,300	10,705	397
39	39	1,630.20	35	.1472	73.33	2,860	1,630	903
48,194		1,204,947.43	24,822	3.10874	36.29	1,749,064	1,163,665	44,832

b = Equation value of per pupil cost of transportation.

minimum program of educational need of a county is defined in terms of weighted pupils or weighted teachers. These units can be converted into dollars. Mort, in a recent unpublished study, found the cost of a weighted pupil in an average community in Pennsylvania to be $46.88. This figure is weighted according to the cost of living of the various communities,[3] as it is applied to the distribution of aid. However, cost of living has already been allowed for by the scheme developed in this study so, in order to determine the number of weighted pupils in the transportation program, merely divide the proposed state aid for transportation in dollars by $46.88 and the quotient is the number of weighted pupils for transportation need that are to be lumped with the rest of the weighted pupil units of educational need for a county. This division was done and the number of weighted pupils for each county reported in Table 4.

State aid for transportation distributed according to this plan will be in the nature of refund in that the aid is always computed for the current year on the basis of the transportation of the preceding year. It will be observed that the state's participation in the transportation program for Pennsylvania for 1928 is computed on the basis of data for 1925-1926 and 1926-1927. The numbers transported and cost of transportation were unfortunately not available for 1926-1927. These calculations illustrate the use of the technique but the actual apportionment of state aid for 1928 should be done on the basis of data for 1926-1927.

VARIATION IN DISTANCES TRANSPORTED

Another problem presenting itself is that if transportation is not compulsory, but is merely permissive in a state, counties will vary in the distances children must live from school before transportation is furnished. Studies in Florida which are presented later in this study show that counties vary from 1 to 3 miles in the minimum distances children must live from school before public transportation is provided. Reavis,[4] in a study conducted in Maryland, reported the following:

In the absence of transportation, distance is the strongest single factor influencing the attendance of country children. It decreases with each age group, the correlation being about .60 for 5 to 7 year old children, .45 for

---

[3] Harry, D. P., Jr., *Cost of Living of Teachers in the State of New York.*
[4] Reavis, G. H., *Factors Controlling Attendance in Rural Schools*, p. 13.

8 to 11, and .25 for 12 and over. Children living more than 2 miles from school attend only half as many days as children living within a quarter of a mile of school.

Here are some problems of distance that need further research before they can be decided upon the basis of objective evidence.

1. What is a reasonable walking distance for different age groups?

2. Is a reasonable walking distance uniform in all situations in the state?

3. What is an unreasonable riding distance? Obviously, in computing the minimum program for transportation, inequalities will likely be introduced if counties are not placed on an equitable basis as far as distance is concerned. In the absence of objective evidence as to variations in the need of different communities to transport children different distances in order to furnish equivalent educational offering, it would seem at present desirable for the state to set tentative uniform minimum distances for different age groups for communities to transport children and count transportation above these distances within the minimum program. That is, if a state sets the minimum distance for children 5 to 7 years of age at 1 mile, 8 to 11 years at 1½ miles, and 12 years and above at 2 miles, it does not mean that a community cannot transport children living lesser distances from school but that the state will include in its minimum program only children transported the minimum distances or above.

When the State Should Refuse to Give Aid for Transportation

The fourth criterion of the elements that should be included in the minimum program proposed by Mort and quoted in Chapter II of this study, asserts that no element should be included in the minimum program whose harm outweights its benefit. This at once suggests that the state should not promote transportation in vehicles which are unsafe or uncomfortable, or which do not protect the children from inclement weather.

Who Should Be the Local Administrator of Transportation?

The responsibility of approving the transportation provided can perhaps be most conveniently delegated to the county superintendent. He should be directly responsible for the local administration of transportation in states where the county unit is the local unit and, in states where the county is a sort of intermediary unit, the county superintendent will be a general supervisor of transportation in his county, approving, reporting, and advising on transportation.

In states where the county is not the local unit and the state department is faced with the necessity of computing the educational need for smaller units than the county, two plans are feasible: (1) Divide the aid on a pro rata basis in each county or some other political division among the several districts according to the number each is transporting, or (2) compute the transportation need in terms of local districts in exactly the same manner as if they were counties. This is shown to be feasible in the next chapter, the transportation need curve and regression lines for cost being computed for the state of Connecticut by towns which have an average area of only 29.374 square miles.

In states where the county is the unit, the administration of funds locally could well be left entirely in the hands of the county superintendent.

APPLICATION OF PROPOSED PLAN

The scheme for distributing state aid for transportation presented in this study was devised especially to be used in connection with Mort's plan for state support. However, it could well be used by states who have not yet committed themselves to a complete program of state support. The state aid for transportation could be distributed directly to the several administrative units on the basis herein proposed, but it would be better to combine it with some measure of taxpaying ability of the various communities.

COMPUTED MINIMUM PROGRAM ONLY A BASIS OF ESTABLISHING A MINIMUM

It is not intended that the minimum program for transportation for a state as computed by these techniques be the actual minimum used. The minimum program as suggested only places all the local communities relatively on the same basis. The state can use any desired minimum it chooses by simply multiplying the minimum as calculated by an appropriate fraction or integer in order to decrease or increase the minimum as desired. The minimum will remain on the same relative base. Thus if a state desires to increase the minimum 25 per cent, all that is necessary is to multiply the calculated minimum for each county or other unit by 1.25.

The final problem which demands an answer is: For how long are the curve for per cent to be transported within the minimum and the regression lines for cost valid? As the average daily attendance of the county increases, the minimum will rise. But it is quite possible that over the entire state an increasing or decreasing percentage of the average daily attendance may be transported in the succeeding years. In that case, the curve would be under or over the actual data and it would produce an under or over statement of the minimum. This can be checked up easily, however, by merely plotting the average per cent transported for the different density groups and testing their departure from the curve. If the relative increase or decrease over the entire state is the same, the plotted values will arrange themselves in a broken curve of the same general shape as the predicted curve but under or above it. If the actual values are, as an example, 10 per cent above or below the equation values, then the equation values can be used by adding or subtracting 10 per cent of each value to or from the value. In case communities of different densities increase the percentage they transport in different proportions, the curve can be fitted again but, as will be shown in the next chapter, the adjustment of the constants to take care of this variation is a relatively simple process, and practically as good a fit can be obtained as by the more difficult methods of the calculus.

Adjustments to the regression lines for cost can be made in the same manner. However, the labor of recalculation by the technique of correlations and regressions is relatively insignificant.

Need for a Department of Research

As will be observed in Table 4, there are wide variations among the counties between the actual per cent transported and the minimum program as well as actual cost variations from the predicted costs. In case a county has special conditions over which it has no control, which cause its transportation needs to be different than those of the other counties of similar densities, then that county should be considered as of a density comparable to its needs. It is the duty of the state department of research to discover and verify those variations. Naturally, this could not be done unless a uniform system of accounting and reporting for transportation was in force in all the counties. Later in this study, such a scheme is devised which by the aid of special studies should enable the state department of research to judge concerning this matter. In addition, invaluable assistance could be rendered by making special studies as to methods of transportation, types of vehicles, selection of drivers, contract or district-owned buses, distances to transport, etc.

COMPUTING THE MINIMUM PROGRAM FOR THE LOCAL DISTRICT

In computing the transportation expenditures within the minimum to be allowed each local district within a county to be counted in its total minimum educational program, the following procedure is suggested: If a county is transporting equal to or less than its minimum, allow each district all its expenditures for transportation. If it is transporting more than its minimum, divide the minimum program for the county among the several districts on the pro rata basis according to the amount each is spending.

POSSIBILITY OF EXCEEDING THE MINIMUM

Mort [5] proposes that all the state should be burdened equally to support a minimum educational offering for every child in the state. Thus a community will still have enough untapped resources to exceed the minimum, if it so desires, by an additional local tax. No plan of state support should render a community powerless to increase its offering nor should it even encourage a uniform offering other than to see that every child is guaranteed at least a minimum. Neither should the aid be administered in such a manner as to perpetuate a bad system of local districtation where it exists, but rather it should render the community more flexible to change. Mort has recognized this principle in his work on state support. It is believed that the method of distributing aid presented in this study will facilitate this objective.

5 Mort, P. R., *State Support for Public Schools,* p. 26.

If aid was distributed only on the basis of teacher units or weighted pupil units per school, without the inclusion of aid for transportation, a given territory would receive more aid comparatively if it had a large number of small schools which have a fewer number of weighted pupils per teacher. This would have a tendency to discourage consolidation. But if, as soon as a school is dissolved, the aid which originally was received on the basis of teacher units is received in the form of transportation aid, the total aid is kept approximately constant. It might be suggested that a community would need less aid if a group of schools were consolidated, but experience has shown that consolidated schools cost as much or more than the one-room rural schools they replace.

If full aid for all transportation was given, it would be possible for a county to embark upon a reckless and perhaps ill-advised program of consolidation. This is avoided by the state including only the minimum transportation program in its support. The community is left free to go ahead on its own initiative and consolidate with its resultant transportation beyond the minimum if it so desires. When the experience of the state has shown its advisability by the raising of the average of the per cent of the average daily attendance transported, then the minimum will be raised, thereby encouraging the counties to move in the direction experience shows advisable for the provision of the best educational offering possible per dollar of money expended for education.

Thus the conditions of a desirable program of state support for transportation as laid down in Chapter III are fulfilled. The validity of the procedure is further substantiated by the application of the proposed technique to four other states in the succeeding chapter.

CHAPTER VI

MEASUREMENT OF THE TRANSPORTATION NEED IN THE STATES OF ALABAMA, CONNECTICUT, FLORIDA, AND NEW JERSEY

Variation of Selected States in Local Conditions

The five states for which the transportation need is calculated in this study were selected because they present a range of widely different situations, and because of availability of data. Table 5 shows that the states selected vary in number of administrative units from 21 counties in New Jersey to 169 towns in Connecticut. The average area of administrative unit varies from approximately 27 square miles in Connecticut to 817 in Florida. The density of school population on the basis of average

TABLE 5

Number of Local Units, Average Area per Local Unit and Density of the Five States Selected

State	Number of Units	Average Area per Unit	Average Daily Attendance per Square Mile
Connecticut	169	27.374	51.52606
Pennsylvania	67	669.134	28.91876
New Jersey	21	357.810	73.87786
Florida	67	817.200	2.65946
Alabama	67	765.350	1.73625

daily attendance per square mile ranges from approximately 1.7 in Alabama to 73.9 in New Jersey. There is a wide variation in climatic conditions in the southern and northern states. The presence of the negro complicates the situation in the south.

The problem is to test the applicability to other states of the curve and regression technique developed for the distribution of state aid for transportation in Pennsylvania.

The state of Florida was studied next. The data necessary,

as in the case of Pennsylvania, were average daily attendance, area of the administrative units, number of students transported, and total cost of transportation. These data are relatively easy to collect for most states, but accurate cost figures for transportation are difficult to secure, as will be shown in a later chapter, unless a uniform accounting system is in use in the entire state. These errors, however, are not constant, and the fluctuations tend to neutralize each other when regression lines are fitted.

Transportation of white children only is considered in this study, because the transportation of colored children is not general in Florida. It is entirely consistent with the principles advanced in this study for the state to allow aid for the transportation of colored children where this is being attempted.

The average per cent transported was first calculated by density groups, as in the case of Pennsylvania. The calculations are reported in Table 9. Then the Pennsylvania equation for the prediction of the minimum program in terms of numbers to be transported was applied to the Florida data. It is shown plotted in Plate 2. An examination of the graph reveals some interesting things about the amount of transportation being done in the different communities of the same density in the two states. It appears as though the two states transport approximately the same percentage of the average daily attendance in the sparsest communities, but Pennsylvania has no counties as sparsely settled as some of the Florida counties. Following the curve up the lowest densities which are present in both states, it is seen that Florida is transporting a considerably higher per cent of its average daily attendance for counties of the same density than is Pennsylvania. It is also observed that the curve does not fall nearly so rapidly in Florida, as it passes from counties of low density to higher density. This may be due to the fact that the climate being milder, transportation over longer distances is feasible in Florida. It may be due to the fact that Florida has the county unit type of organization which enables consolidations to be formed more easily which would tend to increase the amount of transportation. Whatever the cause, transportation as it is being done in a state is the minimum program of transportation for that state and one has no right to force the procedure of one state upon another. Florida is presenting a type of educational offering which demands different percentages of the average daily attendance to be transported than in communities of the same density in Pennsylvania, and the problem is to write the relationship which exists between per cent of average daily attendance transported and density of school population for Florida.

DEVELOPMENT OF INDICES FOR EACH STATE

Two lines of attack are open. One is to proceed as in the case of Pennsylvania, and by the methods of calculus determine the line of best fit. This method, of course, involves considerable labor and an elementary knowledge of calculus. The other method is that of approximation. This method, while a little less refined, requires only a knowledge of elementary algebra and analytical geometry. The second method was selected because of its simplicity and to demonstrate its use. The fit can always be tested and, if it satisfies the conditions laid down in Chapter III, its equation will be satisfactory.

The process is as follows: Observe the deficiencies of the Pennsylvania curve, as shown in Plate 2. As has already been mentioned, it falls too rapidly and goes under the broken line which represents the actual data. The general function $Y = \dfrac{A}{X + K} + B$ has the following properties:

1. If K is made very small, the line will have a steep slope downward as it passes into the first quadrant.

2. If either A or B is increased, the whole line will then be lifted.

3. If A is increased, the line will be lifted proportionately higher for small than for large values of X.

4. If B is increased, the line will be lifted proportionately higher for large than for small values of X.

5. The whole line can be shifted to the left of the reader by increasing the value of K.

6. Shifting the line to the left of the reader reduces the slope of the line for positive values of X and, consequently, when it is made to enter the first quadrant at the same point on the Y axis as before, the predicted values of Y decrease more slowly, thus lifting the line until high values of X are reached.

Knowing these facts about this function enables one with a little practice to obtain a fairly good fit within about an hour's time, once the data are plotted and the equation of another state is available, preferably a state having smiliar conditions.

The deficiencies of the Pennsylvania curve are first attacked by moving the line to the left, adding 5 to X instead of 2. In order to cause the line to enter the first quadrant where the actual data are located, A must be increased to 176, and, in order to keep the line down to the data for large values of X, B is reduced to .5. The plotted curve now looks like a good fit, but the eye should not be trusted, so a test should be tried. The method of Chapter III was again applied and the test r was found to be .85410, which is a high test but not so high as in the case of Pennsylvania. The fact that it is possible to obtain a high test fit is additional evidence that density of school population and per cent of average daily attendance transported are highly associated. It was found profitable later in the study to select the known equation of a state similar to the one being studied as a starting point in fitting the curve. It will quite likely approximate a fit to start the process.

The per pupil costs are calculated by the methods of Chapter IV and the regression lines are shown in Plate 10. The minimum program and proposed state aid are computed for Florida in Table 11.

The same techniques are used in computing the curves for the prediction of per cent to be transported and the regression lines for cost for Connecticut, New Jersey, and Alabama. The reader is cautioned again against judging the fit of a line or curve by its conformity to plotted points on the graph, for these points contain different numbers of frequencies and are therefore of varying importance, although they appear to be of equal value from the graph. The fit of the lines and curves should be judged by the test which is reported on each graph.

The test fits for the different equations for the different states are given in Table 6. The tests are lower for New Jersey than for the other states because there are only 21 counties in New Jersey and it was not possible to find group averages, which fluctuate less than individual cases. Data for 1924 were used for the State of New Jersey so that the reader can compare

TABLE 6

TEST OF FIT FOR THE PREDICTION EQUATIONS FOR THE FIVE STATES

State	Equations for the Prediction of State's Minimum Transportation Program in Terms of Pupils to be Transported	Cost Prediction Equations
Alabama	.88335	.94239
Connecticut	.97394	.89754
Florida	.85410	.89325
New Jersey	.81643	.6894
Pennsylvania	.9697	.95261

the results with Burns' figures which are also reported in Table 6.

It is interesting to note that the fit for Connecticut is quite as good as for the other states even though the town with an average area of only about 27 square miles is used as the unit.

As has been pointed out earlier in this study, a high test fit depends upon the accuracy of the fitting and the association of the two variables. No matter how good a job of fitting is done with this type of function, a good test will not be shown unless the variables are highly associated. The lowest test is that of the cost regression lines for New Jersey which show an r of .6894. If the aid was apportioned on the basis of the average cost per pupil for the whole state, a zero test fit would result. Any value of r above zero is therefore better than the average method of apportioning aid. The fact that the tests for both predictions are high substantiates the hypothesis that per cent of the average daily attendance transported and cost per pupil are both highly associated with density. Density of school population is therefore a valid predictive criterion of per cent of average daily attendance transported and per pupil cost of transportation.

A better test for fit of the lines for cost for some of the states could perhaps be obtained by the use of curves. The curve has the advantage that it is more compact for use, for one has only one equation. Another advantage is that there are no abrupt breaks from one portion of the prediction to the other. This is more likely consistent with the facts, for costs for different densities show considerable overlapping. The fit of a curve could be approximated by the use of a series of regression lines. Only two lines were used in this study because a good fit was obtained in Pennsylvania by this technique and it was desired to use the same technique for cost comparisons among the states as is shown in Plate 13.

The five equations for the prediction of the per cent of the average daily attendance transported as related to density of school population for the states of Pennsylvania, Alabama, Connecticut, Florida, and New Jersey are shown plotted on the same graph in Plate 12. This technique of comparison shows some extremely interesting facts concerning the relative amounts of transportation carried on by these states in presenting their educational offerings. In reading this graph, it is the vertical distances between the lines at the same density which are significant. Speaking in terms of analytical geometry, the ordinary values for each state are compared for the corresponding abscissae values.

It will be observed that Connecticut and New Jersey have quite similar curves, thus indicating that they are transporting about the same proportion of their children in communities of the same density. Florida and Alabama also show quite similar practices. One would expect Pennsylvania to approximate New Jersey and Connecticut more nearly in its transportation policies than Florida and Alabama because of climatic, industrial, and social similarities. But the reverse is true. It was thought at one time in this study that a curve would be desirable combining the evidence from all these states and reporting it as the average experience of the states with respect to the amount of transportation found desirable in communities of varying densities. But the evidence presented in Plate 12 substantiates the statement made earlier in this chapter that each state has its own minimum program of transportation consistent with the other features of its educational program due to differences in administrative organization, climatic conditions, road development, topography of the state, racial problems, and policies of the educational leaders. The question of which state is right in its policies is a problem for further research. The criterion, of which state has the best solution in a group of states with similar conditions and making equal effort, would be which state is getting the greatest return per educational dollar expended. This is glibly said, but its application is a long and tedious task requiring years of research. It might be suggested that the state should distribute aid for transportation on the basis of evaluation of the educational return obtained by the different counties with different policies with respect to transporting pupils. This, again, would be difficult of objective evaluation and would likely involve reward for effort. The state cannot aid transportation until it is carried on, and one could hardly advocate that the state should pay for all the transportation done by all of the communities. This would tend to make the local community irresponsible for its blunders, for the state would assume the burden of hasty and ill-advised consolidations and needless transportation.

Pennsylvania's low percentage of transportation as compared with Connecticut and New Jersey suggests another research problem. Pennsylvania has hundreds of little mining towns scattered over the state. It is possible that a county could have a low density but have practically all of its population in a few centers, and thus its transportation need be relatively small as compared with agricultural counties of the same density. A correction could readily be applied to this scheme as suggested by simply weighting the $\breve{Y}_p$ proportionately and extending or reducing the minimum. Pennsylvania's low position on the graph could be partly due to this cause. It would be a comparatively simple matter for the state bureau of research to investigate the per cent transported in counties of the same density with respect to per cent of rural population. It might be possible to use per cent of rural population as the independent predictive variable.[1] Several difficulties present themselves in this scheme, however. Parochial schools take care of much of the rural and urban population in many states. Accurate census data are obtainable with respect to rural population in many states only once in ten years. It might be suggested that the per cent the average daily attendance of rural population is of the total average daily attendance could be used as the predictive variable. In order to do this, it would be necessary for the state to have the average daily attendance of each child in the state by residence as well as by schools. That is, the state would have to assign the portion of the average daily attendance of each town or city that is made up of rural non-

[1] The writer in a recent unpublished study has applied this predictive variable to data from Nebraska with fair results.

resident or boarded pupils to the rural portions of the county or other administrative unit. These data were not available for the testing of the hypothesis, although it would be possible for the state department to collect such information.

ANALYSIS OF VARIATIONS BETWEEN STATES

Per pupil cost comparisons for transportation for the five states are presented in Plate 13. It is interesting to note that the three states, New Jersey, Pennsylvania and Connecticut, are fairly similar, and Florida and Alabama approach each other. Most public school transportation is now done by motor bus and the salary of the driver is one-half or a little more than one-half of the expense. Wages and cost of living are somewhat lower in the southern states, especially in the rural sections, and this is to be expected. It is possible that other factors influence this cost, such as efficiency of management, type of vehicles provided, condition of the roads, climate, etc.

Another point brought out by this graph which is significant is that costs at first go down as one passes from communities of low to higher densities, but when they reach a low point in Pennsylvania, Florida, and Alabama, they tend to rise somewhat again in the communities of higher density. In Connecticut and New Jersey, costs continue to decrease but at a much less rate. A possible explanation of the fact that costs continue to decrease and reach their lowest point in the communities of highest density in New Jersey and Connecticut is that these states are so densely populated that many public service lines are available for the transportation of school children from which very reasonable contract rates can be secured. The evidence from Pennsylvania discredits this hypothesis slightly for its costs go up a little in the communities of higher density, but not so markedly as to disprove the explanation. It is barely possible that part of these cost variations is due to fluctuations in reporting, which were not smoothed out by averaging, due to the small numbers of frequencies in the communities of higher density. These denser communities, however, transport relatively more of their pupils by contract than by district-owned buses and, as is shown later in this study, reporting for contract transportation is more likely to be accurate than for transportation by district-owned buses.

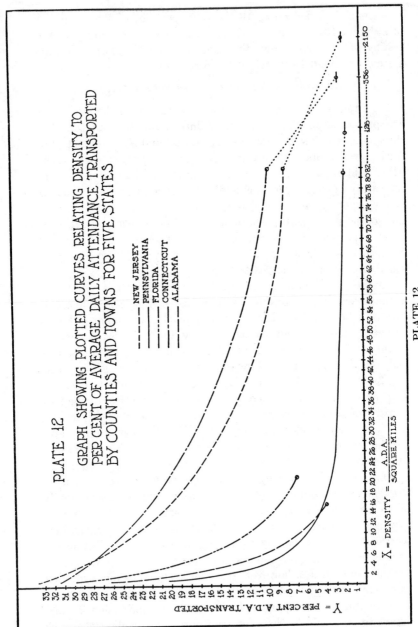

PLATE 12

GRAPH SHOWING PLOTTED CURVES RELATING DENSITY TO
PER CENT OF AVERAGE DAILY ATTENDANCE TRANSPORTED
BY COUNTIES AND TOWNS FOR FIVE STATES

NEW JERSEY
PENNSYLVANIA
FLORIDA
CONNECTICUT
ALABAMA

Y = PER CENT A.D.A. TRANSPORTED

$X = \text{DENSITY} = \dfrac{\text{A.D.A.}}{\text{SQUARE MILES}}$

PLATE 12

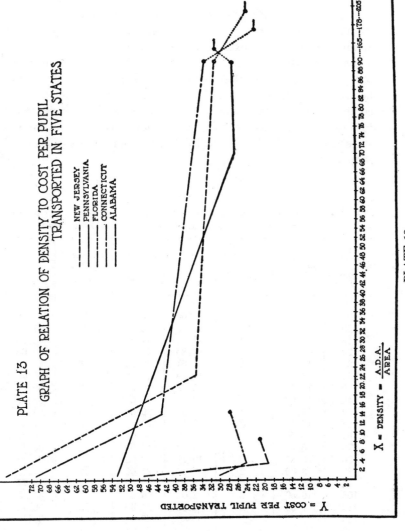

PLATE 13

GRAPH OF RELATION OF DENSITY TO COST PER PUPIL
TRANSPORTED IN FIVE STATES

NEW JERSEY
PENNSYLVANIA
FLORIDA
CONNECTICUT
ALABAMA

X = DENSITY = A.D.A. / AREA

Y = COST PER PUPIL TRANSPORTED

PLATE 13

Still another explanation, and one which is of concern to the state in its equalization program, is that the densest communities might be reporting higher costs due to providing palatially appointed buses more expensive than is requisite for the comfort and safety of the children, while the sparsely settled communities are providing more modest vehicles. Obviously, the state should not recognize costs beyond those necessary to provide safe and comfortable transportation. An investigation in Florida failed to disclose such variations in local policy, but it is well for the state department of research to be aware of such variations if they exist.

TABLE 7

COMPUTATION OF A SMOOTHED CURVE AND REGRESSION LINES FOR THE DETERMINATION OF TRANSPORTATION NEED IN CONNECTICUT

X Density and Points in Intervals of 6	Y_p Average Per Cent Transported	Number of Towns Included in Average	$\tilde{Y}_p$	Y_c Average Cost per Pupil	Number of Towns Included in Average	$\tilde{Y}_c$
4	27.78	50	29.00	$66.96	50	$64.00
10	27.15	31	25.13	48.06	31	51.61
16	25.07	14	22.18	41.47	15	42.76
22	18.73	13	19.84	45.62	13	42.00
28	18.90	5	18.54	42.20	5	41.22
34	16.50	3	16.39	46.00	3	40.46
40	13.50	3	15.08	34.00	3	39.69
46	14.00	4	13.96	50.00	4	38.92
52	11.75	4	13.00	39.00	4	38.15
58	16.50	3	12.16	28.67	3	37.38
64	8.50	3	11.42	38.00	3	36.62
70	6.75	4	10.77	43.00	4	35.85
76	15.00	2	10.19	60.00	2	35.08
82	3.00	2	9.67	24.00	2	34.31
94	15.00	2	8.67	24.00	2	32.77
106	10.50	2	8.02	36.00	2	31.23
112	7.50	2	7.69	24.00	2	30.46
130				25.41	1	28.16
136				51.94	1	27.39
142				39.82	1	26.62
148				53.25	1	25.85
178				21.44	12	22.00
355	2.90	21	2.90			
Total		168			164	

SUMMARY

1. The function developed for Pennsylvania to predict the state's minimum program of transportation can be applied to other states with fair results by the method of approximations.

2. Regression lines can be used for cost predictions in other states, but curves could be used with profit in some cases.

3. High associations of density of school population with per cent of average daily attendance transported and cost per pupil transported are indicated substantiating the use of density of school population as an independent variable for the purposes of prediction.

4. Evidence indicates that different states have different minimum programs for transportation, and each must be calculated with respect to the individual state.

5. Cost fluctuations are marked, but show a similar general trend in states with similar conditions.

6. Further research is necessary to determine the need for a correction to be applied to $\tilde{Y}_p$ (per cent of average daily attendance transported within the minimum program) with respect to per cent of rural population and cost fluctuations due to local policy.

TABLE 8

COMPUTATION OF PER CENT TRANSPORTED CURVE AND COST REGRESSION LINES FOR ALABAMA

X Density Step Mid-Point	f Number of Counties	Y_p Per Cent Trans- ported	Y_p	X Density Step Mid-Point	Y_c Cost per Pupil	f Number of Counties	Y_c
.5	1	22.00	30.29	.5	$56.00	1	46.0722
1.5	9	23.33	23.11	1.5	39.56	9	37.2196
2.5	10	19.70	18.55	2.5	23.78	9	28.3668
3.5	4	5.00	15.38	3.5	14.00	2	19.5144
4.5	9	13.00	13.07				
5.5	9	12.00	11.29	8.5	21.11	29	21.11
6.5	11	10.18	9.89				
8.5	7	15.43	7.83				
15.5	7	4.23	4.11				
Total ...	67					50	

TABLE 9

COMPUTATION OF CURVE FOR PER CENT TRANSPORTED AND REGRESSION
LINES FOR COST PER PUPIL FOR FLORIDA

X Density Step Mid-Point	f Number of Counties	Y_p Per Cent Transported	Y_p	X Density Step Mid-Point	f Number of Counties	Y Cost per Pupil	Y_c Cost per Pupil
.5	9	31.67	32.50	.5	5	$31.36	$29.80
1.5	20	27.75	27.58	1.5	16	29.15	30.00
2.5	15	27.53	23.97	2.5	15	26.92	26.87
3.5	7	19.00	21.21	3.5	6	24.70	22.33
4.5	7	16.14	19.03	4.5	7	22.48	23.29
5.5	1	19.00	17.26	14.5	9	27.89	27.89
7.5	3	19.00	14.58				
9.5	1	11.00	12.64				
10.5	1	11.00	11.85				
13.5			10.01				
16.5			8.69				
19.5			7.68				
21.5	3	6.85	7.14				

Table 8 shows the calculations of the transportation need and cost prediction equations for Alabama. It will be observed that only 50 counties were used in the computation of the cost equations. Those counties transporting very small numbers of students were not included because cost figures on such a basis are not representative of what transportation should cost in counties with their conditions. That is, enough transportation must be done in any county to sample conditions as they exist in order to be indicative of what transportation should cost a county due to factors beyond its control.

The computation of the prediction equations for Connecticut is shown in Table 7. Four towns are omitted in the cost calculations because of inadequacies of the data.

Table 10 shows the application of the techniques to Alabama counties. Tables 12 and 13 show the application to New Jersey and Connecticut, respectively. It will be observed that the total amount of calculation necessary, after the prediction equations are determined, is relatively small. The job can be done by secretarial help of a quality ordinarily obtainable in state department offices. In fact the calculation of Tables 10, 11, 12, and 13 was done by a secretary according to a set-up given by the writer. It was not necessary to acquaint her with the principles involved.

CALCULATION OF THE COST OF THE MINIMUM PROGRAM OF TRANSPORTATION
FOR THE STATE OF

County	A. D. A.	Number Transported	Y_p Per Cent A. D. A. Transported	Area in Square Miles	$\dfrac{\text{A. D. A.}}{\text{Area}}$	Total Cost
Autauga	1,639	427	26.05	584	2.80651	$9,219
Baldwin	3,747	781	20.84	1,595	2.34922	13,890
Barbour	2,537	512	20.18	912	2.78179	13,581
Bibb	2,561	60	2.34	634	4.03943	620
Blount	3,898	167	4.28	649	6.00616	2,112
Bullock	863	291	33.71	610	1.41475	16,225
Butler	4,109	400	9.73	763	5.38532	5,868
Calhoun	7,102	876	12.33	616	11.52922	16,413
Chambers	5,401	1,277	23.64	612	8.28516	27,303
Cherokee	2,972	150	5.04	577	5.15077	3,207
Chilton	3,409	927	27.19	713	4.78120	14,236
Choctaw	1,824	190	10.41	932	1.95708	6,196
Clarke	2,669	539	20.19	1,216	2.19490	14,563
Clay	2,640	375	14.20	614	4.29967	5,981
Cleburne	2,137	60	2.80	569	3.75571	300
Coffee	4,508	241	5.34	678	6.64896	3,584
Colbert	3,747	205	5.47	618	6.06311	15,129
Conecuh	2,414	373	15.45	849	2.84334	9,176
Coosa	1,647	516	31.34	655	2.51450	13,593
Covington	5,675	227	4.00	1,042	5.44625	3,191
Crenshaw	3,726	161	4.32	618	6.02913	2,521
Cullman	6,708	171	2.54	763	8.79161	2,027
Dale	3,690	348	9.43	563	6.55417	4,826
Dallas	2,855	0	0	957	2.98328	0
DeKalb	6,513	213	3.27	786	8.28625	1,777
Elmore	3,615	584	13.41	638	5.66614	8,229
Escambia	3,355	296	8.82	957	3.50574	5,431
Etowah	8,317	692	8.32	539	15.24304	8,576
Fayette	3,689	716	19.40	643	5.73716	12,024
Franklin	3,888	822	21.14	647	6.00927	5,790
Geneva	3,818	0	0	578	6.60554	0
Greene	665	64	9.62	635	1.04724	2,673
Hale	1,425	254	17.82	646	2.20588	3,938
Henry	2,156	160	7.42	560	3.85000	1,110
Houston	5,193	93	1.79	579	8.96891	1,901
Jackson	5,336	225	4.21	1,140	4.68070	3,673
Jefferson	47,631	3,250	6.82	1,120	42.52767	65,725
Lamar	2,786	658	23.61	601	4.63560	10,425
Lauderdale	6,286	125	1.98	694	9.05763	10,255
Lawrence	3,105	4	.01	700	4.43571	81
Lee	3,493	693	19.83	608	5.74506	21,290
Limestone	4,111	0	0	596	6.89765	0
Lowndes	735	165	22.44	739	.99445	9,417
Macon	923	293	31.74	614	1.50325	9,637
Madison	6,696	2,590	38.67	811	8.25647	26,927
Marengo	2,137	670	31.35	966	2.21221	16,804
Marion	4,471	447	9.99	743	6.01749	4,919
Marshall	5,903	33	.55	602	9.80564	135
Mobile	10,711	1,498	13.98	1,226	8.73654	32,592
Monroe	3,189	53	1.66	1,012	3.15118	14,142
Montgomery	7,153	1,696	23.71	801	8.93008	34,882
Morgan	6,443	38	.58	587	10.97614	3,674
Perry	1,026	164	15.98	737	1.39213	9,020
Pickens	2,479	313	12.62	875	2.83314	9,426
Pike	3,246	671	20.67	671	4.83755	6,199
Randolph	3,897	574	14.72	590	6.60508	6,903
Russell	836	176	21.05	655	1.27633	9,392
Shelby	3,288	452	13.74	819	4.01465	5,858
St. Clair	3,348	662	19.77	648	5.16666	10,750
Sumter	1,217	377	30.97	908	1.34030	15,931
Talladega	4,665	1,625	34.83	755	6.17880	22,245
Tallapoosa	3,918	382	9.74	763	5.13499	12,973
Tuscaloosa	6,509	658	10.10	1,346	4.83580	21,066
Walker	8,584	10	.01	792	10.83838	220
Washington	1,545	420	27.18	1,087	1.42134	8,055
Wilcox	1,303	370	28.39	896	1.45424	9,430
Winston	3,262	128	3.92	630	5.17777	3,042
STATE	295,344	32,489	11.00	51,279	1.73625	$670,299

*Data furnished by the Department of Education of the State of Alabama for the year

of Pupils and the Distribution of State Aid for Transportation
Alabama (1926–1927)*

Y_e Cost per Pupil	$\tilde{Y}_p$ Per Cent A. D. A. Transported	Minimum Transportation Program in Pupils	$\tilde{Y}_c$ Cost per Pupil	Outside Cost of Minimum Program if All Counties Transported Up to Minimum	Number of Students for Whom Aid is Allowed	Calculated Cost for Transportation Within the Minimum	Proposed State Aid
$21.59	17.46091	286	$26.57	$7,599	286	$7,599	$7,599
17.78	19.12457	717	30.47	21,847	717	21,847	13,890
26.53	17.54412	445	26.78	11,917	445	11,917	11,917
10.33	14.05244	360	19.69	7,088	60	1,181	620
12.65	10.54697	411	20.31	8,347	167	3,392	2,112
55.76	23.59601	204	38.44	7,842	204	7,842	7,842
14.67	11.47593	472	20.12	9,497	400	8,049	5,868
18.74	7.57743	538	21.01	11,303	538	11,303	11,303
21.38	8.01315	433	21.04	9,110	433	9,110	9,110
21.38	11.86372	353	20.04	7,074	150	3,006	3,006
15.36	12.52218	427	19.92	8,506	427	8,506	8,506
32.61	20.79566	379	33.81	12,814	190	6,424	6,196
27.02	19.75210	527	31.78	16,748	527	16,748	14,563
15.71	13.48015	356	19.77	7,038	356	7,038	5,981
5.00	14.72659	315	19.60	6,174	60	1,176	300
14.87	9.71111	438	20.52	8,988	241	4,945	3,584
73.80	10.46813	392	20.33	7,969	205	4,168	4,168
24.60	17.33825	419	26.26	11,003	373	9,795	9,176
26.34	18.49143	305	29.06	8,863	305	8,863	8,863
14.06	11.37872	646	20.14	13,010	227	4,572	3,191
15.66	10.51505	392	20.32	7,965	161	3,272	2,521
11.85	7.58308	509	21.01	10,694	171	3,593	2,027
13.87	9.82729	363	20.49	7,438	348	7,131	4,826
	16.88596	482	25.06	12,079	0	0	0
8.34	8.81218	574	21.04	12,077	213	4,482	1,777
16.97	11.03925	399	20.21	8,064	399	8,064	8,064
18.35	15.36927	516	19.52	10,072	296	5,778	5,431
12.39	4.19414	349	21.01	7,332	349	7,332	7,332
16.79	10.93326	403	20.23	8,153	403	8,153	8,153
7.04	10.54264	410	20.32	8,332	410	8,332	5,790
	9.76404	373	20.51	7,650	0	0	0
41.77	25.92026	172	41.57	7,150	64	2,660	2,660
15.50	19.70622	281	31.69	8,905	254	8,049	3,938
6.94	14.49635	313	19.63	6,144	160	3,141	1,110
20.33	7.44113	386	21.01	8,110	93	1,954	1,901
16.32	12.71220	678	19.89	13,485	225	4,475	3,673
20.22	4.10811	1,957	21.01	41,117	1,957	41,117	41,117
15.84	12.79910	357	19.88	7,097	357	7,097	7,097
82.04	7.37166	463	21.01	9,728	125	2,626	2,626
20.25	13.19692	410	19.81	8,122	4	79	79
30.72	10.92158	381	20.23	7,708	381	7,708	7,708
	9.41685	387	20.60	7,972	0	0	0
57.07	26.28925	193	42.02	8,108	165	6,933	6,933
32.89	23.09298	213	37.68	8,026	213	8,026	8,026
10.40	8.03867	538	21.03	11,314	538	11,314	11,314
25.08	19.67986	421	31.64	13,320	421	11,320	11,320
11.00	10.53120	471	20.32	9,571	447	9,083	4,919
4.09	6.82423	403	21.01	8,467	33	693	135
21.76	7.62805	817	21.01	17,165	817	16,175	17,165
26.68	16.37045	522	23.63	12,335	53	1,252	1,252
20.57	7.47186	534	21.01	11,219	534	11,219	11,219
96.68	6.08521	392	21.01	8,236	38	798	798
55.00	23.72783	243	38.63	9,387	164	6,335	6,335
30.12	17.27307	431	26.34	11,353	313	8,244	8,244
9.24	12.41777	403	19.94	8,036	403	8,036	6,199
12.03	9.76460	381	20.51	7,814	381	7,814	6,903
53.36	24.42452	204	39.62	8,082	176	6,973	6,973
12.96	14.10914	464	19.68	9,132	452	8,895	5,858
16.24	11.83674	396	20.05	7,940	396	7,940	7,940
42.26	24.03507	293	39.07	11,448	293	11,448	11,448
13.69	10.31098	481	20.37	9,798	481	9,798	9,798
33.96	11.89061	466	20.03	9,334	382	7,651	7,651
32.02	12.42099	808	19.94	16,112	658	13,120	13,120
22.00	6.16569	529	21.01	11,114	10	210	210
19.18	23.55786	364	38.38	13,970	364	13,970	8,055
25.49	23.36908	304	38.10	11,582	304	11,582	9,430
23.77	11.81795	386	20.05	7,739	128	2,566	2,566
20.63				$688,733	$20,845	$494,908	$439,436

1926–1927.

COMPUTATION OF A PROPOSED PROGRAM OF STATE AID FOR SCHOOL

County	A. D. A. White	Number Transported White	Total Cost White	Y_c Cost per Pupil	Area in Square Miles	X $\dfrac{\text{A. D. A.}}{\text{Area}}$	Y_p Per Cent of A. D. A. Transported
Alachua	3,830	1,030	$22,920	$22.25	904	4.23675	26.89295
Baker	849	236	3,593	15.22	593	1.43170	27.79740
Bay	1,755	259	6,348	24.51	781	2.24712	14.75783
Bradford	1,058	225	5,145	22.87	299	3.53846	21.26654
Brevard	2,182	865	35,248	40.75	1,025	2.12878	39.64253
Broward	4,600	543	11,152	20.54	1,212	3.79538	11.80435
Calhoun[a]	882	84	1,069	12.73	568	1.55282	9.52381
Charlotte	612	272	4,671	17.17	776	.78866	44.44444
Citrus	835	158	8,409	53.22	620	1.34677	18.92215
Clay	863	225	6,904	30.68	615	1.40325	26.07184
Collier[a]	236	164	4,884	29.78	1,980	.11919	69.49152
Columbia	1,874	884	17,777	20.11	792	2.36616	47.17182
Dade	20,311	2,489	68,718	27.61	2,019	10.05993	12.25444
DeSoto	1,500	160	5,261	32.88	613	2.44698	10.66667
Dixie[a]	435	27	2,344	86.81	730	.59589	6.20690
Duval	16,736	1,430	59,129	41.35	782	21.40150	8.54446
Escambia	6,141	730	15,097	20.68	657	9.34703	11.88732
Flagler	370	212	7,425	35.02	491	.75356	57.29729
Franklin	565	30	1,098	36.60	541	1.04436	5.30973
Gadsden	2,234	320	7,000	21.88	540	4.13704	14.32408
Gilchrist	565	460	7,119	15.48	353	1.60056	81.41592
Glades[a]	199	54	2,367	43.83	799	.24906	27.13568
Gulf	414	94	2,045	21.76	521	.79463	22.70531
Hamilton	1,238	287	4,931	17.18	528	2.34470	23.18255
Hardee	2,522	384	6,332	16.49	612	4.12092	15.22601
Hendry	345	81	2,442	30.15	1,167	.29563	23.47826
Hernando	898	206	6,926	33.62	497	1.80684	22.93986
Highlands	1,556	250	7,087	28.35	1,044	1.49042	16.06684
Hillsborough	24,280	1,076	27,617	25.67	1,036	23.43629	4.43163
Holmes	2,277	126	3,960	31.43	473	4.81395	5.53360
Indian River	1,097	322	10,041	32.33	521	2.10557	29.84245
Jackson	3,951	757	14,724	19.45	939	4.20767	19.15971
Jefferson	967	515	13,004	25.25	588	1.64456	53.25749
Lafayette	639	268	5,630	21.01	555	1.19887	41.94053
Lake	3,774	981	32,340	32.97	1,047	3.60458	25.99364
Lee	2,466	857	20,414	23.82	884	2.78959	34.75264
Leon	1,612	282	5,899	20.92	715	2.25455	17.49380
Levy	1,512	393	14,424	36.70	1,148	1.31707	25.99206
Liberty	474	7	274	39.14	823	.57594	1.47679
Madison	1,499	474	9,630	20.32	719	2.08484	31.62108
Manatee	3,838	379	10,179	26.86	781	4.91421	9.87493
Marion	3,062	1,079	27,152	24.75	1,647	1.85914	35.23840
Martin	644	247	12,534	50.74	569	1.13181	38.35403
Monroe[a]	1,852	322	9,592	29.79	1,100	1.68364	17.38661
Nassau	1,037	252	7,042	27.94	630	1.64603	24.00867
Oskaloosa	1,719	834	15,251	18.29	956	1.79812	48.51658
Okeechobee	721	227	5,828	25.67	747	.96519	31.48404
Orange	7,392	779	22,403	28.76	929	7.95694	10.53842
Osceola	1,744	379	16,135	42.57	1,356	1.28614	21.73165
Palm Beach	6,708	452	14,252	31.53	1,969	2.40681	6.27081
Pasco	2,016	469	11,196	23.87	767	2.62842	23.26389
Pinellas	11,514	873	23,765	27.22	293	39.29692	7.58207
Polk	13,518	743	24,825	33.41	1,907	7.08862	5.49638
Putnam	2,092	538	12,650	23.51	752	2.78191	25.71702
St. Johns	1,786	420	16,263	38.72	608	2.93750	23.51624
St. Lucie	1,202	325	9,726	29.93	556	2.16187	27.03827
Santa Rosa[b]	2,467	1,329	30,567	23.00	1,025	2.40683	53.87109
Sarasota[a]	2,443	482	11,987	24.87	556	4.39388	19.72984
Seminole	2,483	947	24,192	25.55	321	7.73520	38.13935
Sumter	1,914	371	6,820	18.38	583	3.28302	19.38349
Suwannee[a]	2,588	901	18,550	20.59	692	3.73988	34.81453
Taylor	1,493	399	8,075	27.01	1,045	1.42871	20.02679
Union[a]	944	58	800	13.79	240	3.93333	6.14407
Volusia	6,137	1,093	25,669	23.48	1,123	5.46483	17.81000
Wakulla	740	45	752	16.71	602	1.22924	6.08108
Walton	1,773	87	3,168	36.41	1,095	1.61918	4.90694
Washington[a]	1,904	161	2,690	16.71	620	3.07097	8.45588
STATE	205,884	32,308	863,467	26.73	54,754	2.65946	15.69233

* Data furnished by Florida Department of Education.
[a] Calculated from questionnaire and superintendent's biennial reports.

Transportation for the State of Florida (1926–1927)*

Current Expense	$\tilde{Y}_p$ Per Cent Transported	$\tilde{Y}_c$ Cost per Pupil	Minimum Transportation Program in Terms of Pupils	Maximum Cost of Minimum Program if All Counties Transport up to Minimum	Number of Students Transported Within the Minimum Program	Calculated Cost of Transportation Within the Minimum	Proposed State Aid	Per Cent Cost of Transportation Is of Current Expense
$281,836	19.55436	$24.43	749	$18,298	749	$18,298	$18,298	8.1
35,916	27.86446	29.30	237	6,944	236	6,915	3,593	10.0
100,769	24.78551	27.48	435	11,953	259	7,117	6,438	6.3
152,491	21.11262	24.61	223	5,488	223	5,488	5,145	3.4
256,597	25.18866	27.75	550	15,263	550	12,263	12,263	13.7
1,213,819	20.51051	24.28	943	22,896	543	13,183	11,152	.9
52,136	27.35867	29.03	241	6,996	84	2,439	1,069	2.1
62,879	30.90427	30.73	189	5,808	189	5,808	4,671	7.4
84,379	28.23064	29.49	236	6,960	158	4,659	4,659	9.9
51,149	27.98604	29.36	242	7,105	225	6,606	6,606	13.5
21,552	34.88044	32.21	82	2,641	82	2,641	2,641	22.7
98,894	24.39305	27.22	457	12,440	452	12,303	12,303	18.0
4,057,796	12.18664	26.39	2,475	65,315	2,475	65,315	65,315	1.7
100,190	24.13374	27.04	362	9,788	160	4,326	4,326	5.2
27,990	31.95165	31.15	139	4,330	27	841	841	8.4
1,577,041	7.16663	27.89	1,199	33,440	1,199	33,440	33,440	3.7
377,110	12.76735	26.15	784	20,502	730	19,090	15,097	4.0
37,437	31.08976	30.80	115	3,542	115	3,542	3,542	19.8
26,545	29.61805	30.16	167	5,037	30	905	905	4.1
93,292	19.76226	24.39	441	10,756	320	7,805	7,000	7.5
32,381	27.16440	28.92	153	4,425	153	4,425	4,425	22.0
31,485	34.02981	31.93	68	2,171	54	1,724	1,724	7.5
29,452	30.87295	30.71	128	3,931	94	2,887	2,045	6.9
42,265	24.46286	27.27	303	8,263	287	7,826	4,931	11.7
78,231	19.79630	24.39	499	12,171	384	9,366	6,332	8.1
36,972	33.73495	31.82	116	3,691	81	2,577	2,442	6.6
67,338	26.35634	28.46	237	6,745	206	5,863	5,863	10.3
147,053	27.61689	29.17	430	12,543	250	7,293	7,087	4.8
1,242,186	7.24151	27.89	1,758	49,031	1,076	30,010	27,617	2.2
57,199	18.43366	24.62	420	10,340	126	3,102	3,102	6.9
133,126	25.26930	27.80	277	7,701	277	7,701	7,701	7.5
138,998	19.61450	24.42	775	18,926	757	18,486	14,724	10.6
58,927	26.98783	28.82	261	7,522	261	7,522	7,528	22.1
33,188	28.89227	29.81	185	5,515	185	5,515	5,515	17.0
370,234	18.82459	24.47	710	17,374	710	17,374	17,374	8.7
226,061	23.09426	26.28	570	14,979	570	14,979	14,979	9.0
112,263	24.76064	27.47	399	10,961	282	7,747	5,899	5.3
104,396	28.36102	29.55	429	12,677	393	11,613	11,613	13.8
17,530	32.06418	31.20	152	4,742	7	218	218	1.6
85,550	25.38177	27.84	380	10,579	380	10,579	9,680	11.3
188,679	18.25230	24.66	701	17,287	379	9,346	9,346	5.4
204,370	26.15919	28.35	801	22,708	801	22,708	22,708	13.3
89,331	29.20278	29.96	188	5,632	188	5,632	5,632	14.0
128,798	26.83296	28.74	497	14,284	322	9,254	9,254	7.4
49,470	26.98197	28.82	280	8,070	252	7,263	7,042	14.2
89,296	26.38951	28.48	454	12,930	454	12,930	12,930	17.1
56,786	30.00451	30.33	216	6,551	216	6,551	5,828	10.3
547,205	14.08345	25.68	1,041	26,733	779	20,005	20,005	4.1
156,718	28.49810	29.62	497	14,721	379	11,226	11,226	10.3
975,189	24.26192	27.13	1,627	44,141	452	12,263	12,263	1.5
117,368	23.57162	26.64	475	12,654	469	12,494	11,196	9.5
861,644	4.47319	27.89	834	23,260	834	23,260	23,260	2.8
844,827	15.05915	25.39	2,036	51,694	743	18,865	18,865	2.9
149,492	23.11654	26.29	494	12,724	484	12,724	12,650	8.5
157,750	22.67323	25.95	405	10,510	405	10,510	10,510	10.3
103,266	25.07459	27.67	301	8,329	301	8,329	8,329	9.4
67,332	24.26185	27.13	599	16,251	599	16,251	16,251	95.4
183,399	19.23560	24.48	470	11,506	470	11,506	11,506	6.5
189,136	14.31996	25.61	356	14,470	356	14,470	14,470	12.8
118,126	21.74829	25.18	416	10,475	371	9,342	6,820	5.8
86,570	20.63758	24.26	534	12,955	534	12,955	12,955	21.4
83,742	27.87719	29.30	416	12,189	299	8,761	8,075	9.6
24,902	20.20150	24.33	191	4,647	58	1,411	800	3.2
634,808	21.29191	24.84	1,307	32,466	1,093	27,150	25,669	4.0
18,056	28.75385	29.75	213	6,337	45	1,339	752	4.2
77,040	27.08940	28.88	480	13,862	87	2,512	2,512	4.1
51,333	22.30655	25.65	425	10,901	161	4,130	2,690	5.2
18,009,286			34,761	938,076	26,870	722,978	683,499	4.8

b Data from this County are uncertain. The cost figure is probably accurate, but it is doubtful if the school pays the entire cost of transportation.

TABLE 12

Application of Formulae to Data from New Jersey for the Year 1924, Comparing the Minimum Program and Proposed State Aid as Proposed by the Writer and by Burns*

County	A. D. A.	Per Cent Transported	Density A.D.A. Area	F_p	Cost per Pupil	F_e	Number Transported	Minimum Program in Terms of Pupils Transported	Cost of Minimum Program in Dollars	Number of Transported Pupils for Whom Aid is Allowed	Calculated Cost of Transportation Within Minimum	Total Cost of Transportation	State Aid Proposed	Burns' Minimum Program in Dollars	Burns' Proposed State Aid
Atlantic	16,771	9.421	29.47	15.12442	34.84	35.03	1,580	2,536	88,836	1,580	$55,347	$55,048	$55,048	$93,682.80	$55,047.63
Bergen	49,097	7.723	207.16	4.46707	19.84	24.00	3,792	2,193	52,632	2,193	52,632	75,235	52,632	57,836.20	57,836.20
Burlington	14,086	28.255	17.28	19.57940	27.19	45.74	3,980	2,758	126,151	2,758	126,150	108,208	108,208	120,519.80	108,207.88
Camden	31,384	5.219	141.37	5.67674	36.85	27.89	1,638	1,782	49,700	1,638	45,684	60,356	45,684	50,088.80	50,088.80
Cape May	4,654	15.556	17.56	19.44462	38.33	45.20	724	905	40,906	724	32,725	27,753	27,753	39,307.60	27,753.28
Cumberland	11,597	19.686	23.19	17.08208	29.58	35.43	2,283	1,981	70,187	1,981	70,187	67,522	67,522	78,442.20	67,521.88
Essex	113,745	1.667	895.63	2.23611	30.63	24.00	1,897	2,543	61,032	1,897	45,528	58,103	45,528	43,450.60	43,450.60
Gloucester	10,499	19.678	31.62	14.55695	33.69	34.89	2,066	1,528	53,312	1,528	53,312	69,604	53,312	55,191.60	55,191.60
Hudson	92,444	1.245	2149.86	2.81062	23.99	34.99	1,151	1,674	66,044	1,151	27,624	27,609	27,609	16,824.80	16,824.80
Hunterdon	5,123	11.790	105.01	22.74842	88.61	56.69	604	1,665	49,407	604	34,241	53,519	34,241	59,775.20	53,518.81
Mercer	23,734	9.041	98.14	6.89157	85.64	30.65	2,146	1,636	67,614	1,636	49,407	75,205	49,407	48,037.60	48,037.60
Middlesex	30,621	8.582	44.21	7.38510	29.67	34.92	2,628	2,206	83,388	2,206	67,614	77,967	67,614	65,529.00	65,529.00
Monmouth	21,825	15.492	41.28	11.38841	37.08	40.50	3,331	2,449	86,900	2,449	83,388	123,517	83,388	85,789.00	85,789.00
Morris	21,379	25.924	7.51	14.66149	40.50	64.98	1,241	2,280	75,916	2,174	75,840	92,432	75,916	79,786.20	92,431.02
Ocean	4,787	23.360	230.31	26.00018	40.84	24.00	1,517	1,245	45,432	1,241	36,840	50,687	50,687	79,204.80	42,290.90
Passaic	45,142	25.902	17.74	4.19266	31.34	45.44	1,550	1,893	53,028	1,893	36,408	42,291	36,408	50,816.20	48,579.94
Salem	5,984	11.761	28.43	19.50214	48.05	35.10	1,020	1,167	46,964	1,167	53,028	48,580	48,580	50,816.40	49,011.90
Somerset	8,677	19.720	8.52	15.41699	77.74	62.99	889	1,338	71,368	1,020	35,802	49,012	35,802	49,875.40	68,109.63
Sussex	4,508	3.928	336.53	25.13254	15.81	24.00	1,483	1,133	29,400	889	55,998	68,110	55,998	68,254.40	23,453.44
Union	37,754	11.104	22.61	3.24372	52.47	35.47	909	1,225	50,296	1,225	29,400	23,453	23,453	26,880.80	47,697.02
Warren	8,186			17.31788				1,418		909	32,242	47,697	32,242	56,499.80	
State	555,119	6.97	73.88		33.63		38,709	36,949	$1,302,689	32,487		$1,301,905	$1,077,032	$1,274,816.20	$1,157,059.23

* Data taken from *Measurement of the Need for Transporting Pupils*, by R. L. Burns.

60

TABLE 13

Town	Area in Acres	Number Transported	Total Cost	Average[a] Daily Attendance	Density per Square Mile A. D. A. / Area	Per Cent Transported	Cost per Pupil
Andover	10,452	45	$1,897	76	4.65365	59.21	$42.16
Ansonia	3,715			3,427	590.38493		
Ashford	21,610	38	3,155	154	4.56085	24.68	83.03
Avon	13,292	50	2,089	333	16.03370	15.02	41.78
Barkhamsted	25,093	29	1,319	160	4.08082	18.13	45.48
Beacon Falls	5,792	47	716	334	36.90608	14.07	15.23
Berlin	15,402	149	3,490	1,062	44.12647	14.03	23.42
Bethany	12,735	27	2,422	81	4.07067	33.33	89.70
Bethel	9,918	7	709	555	35.81367	1.26	101.29
Bethlehem	12,698	64	3,700	106	5.34267	60.38	57.81
Bloomfield	17,436	134	4,193	645	23.67515	20.78	31.29
Bolton	9,660	10	288	95	6.29400	10.53	28.80
Bozrah	12,812	16	696	170	8.49204	9.41	43.50
Branford	15,219	189	5,583	1,391	58.49530	13.59	29.54
Bridgeport	11,785	65	4,697	23,148	1257.08270	.28	72.26
Bridgewater	10,201	21	1,674	55	3.45064	38.18	79.71
Bristol	17,278	162	2,607	4,491	166.35258	3.61	16.09
Brookfield	12,749	10	1,000	161	8.08220	6.21	100.00
Brooklyn	18,379	87	5,711	262	9.12346	33.21	65.64
Burlington	20,160	26	1,823	254	8.06349	10.24	70.12
Canaan	26,754	28	1,892	97	2.32040	28.87	67.57
Canterbury	27,882	28	1,587	194	4.45305	14.43	56.68
Canton	19,799	93	3,133	505	16.32406	18.42	33.69
Chaplin	13,689	20	1,380	78	3.64672	25.64	69.00
Cheshire	19,359	236	9,892	441	14.57926	53.51	41.92
Chester	10,338	44	1,001	342	21.17237	12.87	22.75
Clinton	10,524	40	1,681	154	9.36526	25.97	42.03
Colchester	34,131	43	1,360	577	10.81949	7.45	31.63
Colebrook	20,931	63	4,255	116	3.54689	54.31	67.54
Columbia	14,467	36	1,918	157	6.94546	22.93	53.28
Cornwall	31,784	23	2,222	139	2.79889	16.55	96.61
Coventry	24,204	70	3,030	283	7.48306	24.73	43.29
Cromwell	8,455	107	2,643	500	37.84743	21.40	24.70
Danbury	29,047	61	4,175	3,206	70.63862	1.90	68.44
Darien	9,536	271	7,267	876	58.79195	30.94	28.14
Derby	3,293	50	700	1,558	302.79987	3.21	14.00
Durham	15,417	146	3,067	194	8.05345	75.26	21.01
Eastford	18,269	33	1,631	134	4.69429	24.63	49.42
East Granby	11,341	38	2,175	190	10.72216	20.00	57.24
East Haddam	35,712	216	9,007	466	8.35126	46.35	41.70
East Hampton	23,147	154	7,101	387	10.70031	39.79	46.11
East Hartford	11,674	400	8,544	2,900	158.98578	13.79	21.36
East Haven	8,069	215	3,558	1,350	107.07646	15.93	16.55
East Lyme	23,515	106	5,494	370	10.07017	28.65	51.83
Easton	16,279	78	4,497	183	7.19455	42.62	57.65
East Windsor	17,081	253	12,239	737	27.61431	34.33	48.38
Ellington	22,685	55	2,837	419	11.82103	13.13	51.58
Enfield	22,647	388	13,914	2,625	74.18201	14.78	35.86
Essex	7,559	43	2,533	627	53.08639	6.86	58.91
Fairfield	20,560	424	12,056	3,095	96.34241	13.70	28.43
Farmington	15,711	211	7,641	850	34.62542	24.82	36.21
Franklin	12,569	31	2,229	118	6.00843	26.27	71.90
Gastonbury	35,116	210	9,957	1,148	20.92266	18.29	47.41
Goshen	26,542	64	2,830	131	3.15865	48.85	44.22
Granby	26,167	60	3,920	257	6.28578	23.35	65.33
Greenwich	37,346	213	11,365	4,464	104.47451	4.77	53.36
Griswold	23,659	96	5,788	784	21.20800	12.24	59.46
Groton	22,331	72	7,275	1,588	45.51162	4.53	101.04
Guilford	20,139	123	4,079	515	16.36625	23.88	33.16
Haddam	29,375	77	4,472	280	6.10043	27.50	58.08
Hamden	21,054	523	10,172	3,147	95.66258	16.62	19.45
Hampton	16,001	23	2,810	90	3.59978	25.56	122.17
Hartford	11,158	253	4,405	22,197	1314.47210	1.10	17.41

TABLE 13 (*continued*)

Town	Area in Acres	Number Transported	Total Cost	Average^a Daily Attendance	Density per Square Mile A. D. A. / Area	Per Cent Transported	Cost per Pupil
Hartland	22,300	14	$1,874	88	2.52556	15.91	$133.86
Harwinton	20,958	12	1,530	196	5.98530	6.12	127.50
Hebron	22,651	44	3,433	166	4.69030	26.51	78.02
Kent	31,542	21	1,951	188	3.81460	11.17	92.90
Killingly	33,065	101	5,588	1,147	22.20112	8.81	53.33
Killingworth	23,791	11	913	93	2.50179	11.83	83.00
Lebanon	33,800	57	1,782	320	6.05917	17.81	31.26
Ledyard	25,952	36	2,347	178	4.38964	20.22	65.19
Lisbon	10,966	33	1,213	195	11.38063	16.92	36.76
Litchfield	33,065	150	7,028	637	12.32965	23.55	46.85
Lyme	23,564	15	1,327	104	2.82465	14.42	88.47
Madison	25,948	224	4,859	352	8.68198	63.64	21.69
Manchester	17,353	40	2,130	3,956	145.90214	1.01	53.25
Mansfield	29,455	137	5,795	424	9.21270	32.31	42.30
Marlborough	14,774	16	723	49	2.12265	32.65	45.19
Meriden	10,483	188	3,950	5,043	307.88133	3.73	21.01
Middlebury	12,479	44	1,007	205	10.51366	21.46	22.89
Middlefield	8,406	66	2,379	223	16.97835	29.60	36.04
Middletown	27,287	158	5,177	3,431	80.47202	4.61	32.77
Milford	16,290	1	14	2,072	81.40544	.05	14.00
Monroe	15,199	73	5,379	193	8.12685	37.82	73.68
Montville	27,791	133	3,696	815	18.76867	16.32	27.79
Morris	10,397	18	1,325	85	5.23228	21.18	73.61
Naugatuck	10,750	28	1,115	2,378	141.57395	1.18	39.82
New Britain	8,810	82	705	11,370	825.97040	.72	8.60
New Canaan	14,813	135	5,047	888	38.36630	15.20	37.39
New Fairfield	14,982	6	404	88	3.75918	6.82	67.33
New Hartford	24,075	60	4,777	258	6.85857	23.26	79.62
New Haven	14,260			30,036	1348.03920		
Newington	8,794	156	4,280	696	50.65272	22.41	27.44
New London	3,452			3,907	724.35680		
New Milford	40,321	42	3,052	896	14.22187	4.69	72.67
New Town	38,664	75	3,399	410	6.78668	18.29	44.52
Norfolk	29,006	131	9,513	193	4.25843	67.88	72.62
North Branford	16,498	135	4,236	310	12.02570	43.55	31.38
North Canaan	12,480	20	1,080	430	22.05128	4.65	54.00
North Haven	13,890	125	2,900	624	28.75162	20.03	23.20
North Stonington	36,316	5	395	212	3.73609	2.36	79.00
Norwalk	15,777	154	3,657	5,416	219.70209	2.84	23.75
Norwich	18,708	48	2,493	4,035	138.03720	1.19	51.94
Old Lyme	16,893	107	4,670	167	6.32688	64.07	43.64
Old Saybrook	11,561	127	1,915	272	15.05752	46.69	15.08
Orange	11,184	268	5,418	282	16.13734	95.04	20.22
Oxford	23,035	60	4,189	280	7.77947	21.43	69.82
Plainfield	27,119	22	1,850	1,034	24.40208	2.13	84.09
Plainville	6,020	130	2,296	1,077	114.49833	12.07	17.66
Plymouth	13,734	103	4,566	1,440	67.10354	7.15	44.33
Pomfret	27,206	84	6,194	273	6.42211	30.77	73.74
Portland	17,283	37	1,800	591	21.88509	6.26	48.65
Preston	20,325	28	1,707	209	6.58106	13.40	60.96
Prospect	8,726	26	863	111	8.14119	23.42	33.19
Putnam	12,662	21	824	848	42.86211	2.48	39.24
Reddington	20,507	123	7,022	210	6.55386	58.57	57.09
Ridgefield	22,399	181	6,663	675	19.28658	26.81	36.81
Rocky Hill	9,111	75	2,756	404	28.37888	18.57	36.75
Roxbury	17,525	6	179	117	4.27275	5.13	29.83
Salem	18,597	15	557	120	4.12970	12.50	37.13
Salisbury	38,761	65	3,554	437	7.21550	14.87	54.68
Saybrook	9,452	117	2,622	546	36.96995	21.43	22.41
Scotland	12,002	46	3,149	60	3.19947	76.67	68.46
Seymour	9,509	88	2,598	1,477	994.08980	5.96	29.52
Sharon	38,819	146	6,698	251	4.13818	58.17	45.88
Shelton	19,978	249	8,509	2,031	65.06357	12.26	34.17
Sherman	15,041	24	1,480	88	3.74443	27.27	61.67
Simsbury	19,530	10	850	757	24.80686	1.32	85.00
Somers	17,310	82	5,501	417	15.41768	19.66	67.09
Southbury	25,818	24	1,800	181	4.48679	13.26	75.00
Southington	24,310	92	2,380	2,108	55.49650	4.37	25.87

TABLE 13 (*continued*)

Town	Area in Acres	Number Transported	Total Cost	Average[a] Daily Attendance	Density per Square Mile A. D. A. / Area	Per Cent Transported	Cost per Pupil
South Windsor	18,558	360	$10,123	565	19.48486	63.72	$28.12
Sprague	8,620	72	3,522	252	18.70998	28.57	48.92
Stafford	38,495	81	4,786	978	16.25977	8.28	59.09
Stamford	24,430	201	6,532	8,262	216.44207	24.3	32.50
Sterling	17,504	62	3,611	305	11.15174	20.33	58.24
Stonington	25,222	360	13,566	1,708	43.33994	21.08	37.68
Stratford	12,331	93	1,686	3,606	187.15757	2.58	18.13
Suffield	27,349	308	12,053	895	20.94409	34.41	39.13
Thomaston	8,606	50	1,861	822	61.12945	6.08	37.22
Thompston	31,129	182	8,938	647	13.30207	28.13	49.11
Tolland	24,418	45	1,289	197	5.16340	22.84	28.64
Torrington	24,531	9	278	4,272	111.45407	.21	30.89
Trumbull	15,237	194	6,661	593	24.90779	32.72	34.08
Union	18,594	15	1,043	48	1.65215	31.25	69.53
Vernon	11,758	72	1,953	1,240	67.49047	5.81	27.13
Voluntown	25,640	16	1,800	96	2.39626	16.67	112.50
Wallingford	23,933	80	3,438	2,488	66.53240	3.22	42.98
Warren	17,801	23	2,031	60	2.15718	38.33	88.30
Washington	26,959	100	5,770	331	7.85786	30.21	57.70
Waterbury	18,405			15,533	540.13148		
Waterford	25,242	313	8,672	784	19.87798	39.92	27.71
Watertown	18,753	3	135	1,520	51.87437	.20	45.00
Westbrook	11,070	57	3,512	150	8.67209	38.00	61.61
West Hartford	13,994	46	1,169	2,783	127.27740	1.65	25.41
West Haven	6,912	398	3,680	3,917	362.68510	10.16	9.25
Weston	12,804	34	1,753	82	4.09872	41.46	51.56
Westport	13,622	150	5,700	942	44.25782	15.92	38.00
Wethersfield	8,597	123	3,500	927	69.01012	13.27	28.46
Willington	21,753	61	4,074	260	7.64952	23.46	66.79
Wilton	17,602	86	3,041	424	15.41643	20.28	35.36
Winchester	16,268	112	5,112	2,016	793.11530	5.56	45.64
Windham	22,750	84	4,521	949	26.69714	7.85	53.82
Windsor	19,303	244	6,293	1,616	53.57924	15.10	25.79
Windsor Locks	4,675	89	7,500	564	77.21070	15.78	84.27
Wolcott	13,154	33	1,951	216	10.50935	15.28	28.82
Woodbridge	12,758	27	645	242	12.13983	11.16	23.89
Woodbury	23,343	65	1,800	277	7.59457	23.47	27.69
Woodstock	39,911	13	568	310	4.97106	4.19	43.69
STATE	3,177,232	16,305	$621,397	255,796	51.52606	6.37	$38.11

* The transportation and average daily attendance figures were taken from the state superintendent's report for 1925–1926. Areas were taken from the state manual.

[a] The figures for average daily attendance given in the state superintendent's report separate A. D. A. into local and non-local attendance, but not according to total A. D. A. for all children residing in a community regardless of where they attend school. This figure is approximated in this column by adding local A. D. A. to the number of students registered in other districts residing in the local community.

CHAPTER VII

STATUS OF SCHOOL TRANSPORTATION IN FLORIDA

It was thought advisable to make some study of the local problems of administration of school transportation, with a view to promoting effectual coöperation with the state administration in the solution of transportation problems. The state can administer its transportation program intelligently only in the light of the knowledge it possesses of local problems, conditions, and needs. An investigation into just what are the problems, what facts are needed for their solution, and how they can best be secured was quite pertinent at this point. An opportunity afforded itself for doing this in connection with the *Florida State Educational Survey*[1] being conducted by the division of Field Studies of Teachers College, Columbia University.

A personal trip was made to the state in addition to a very extended questionnaire study. It was not hoped to find final solutions to many of the problems, but their presence and possibilities for their solution are indicated.

EARLY HISTORY OF SCHOOL TRANSPORTATION IN FLORIDA

Public transportation of school children is not a new thing in Florida. The minutes of the county superintendents' convention held in 1900 contain considerable arguments, pro and con, concerning the consolidation of schools and the transportation of pupils. Mention is made of transportation of pupils at public expense being carried on in Polk, Volusia, Duval, and Citrus counties.

The Acts of 1889, Chapter 3782, Section 20, Paragraph 5, provided that

School houses shall not be located nearer than three miles to each other unless for some local reason or necessity.

This necessarily curbed the tendency to establish a one-room

[1] Strayer, G. D., Director.

school in every rural community and caused, subsequently, some consolidation of schools already organized. The state superintendent's biennial reports and reports from the county superintendents show that consolidation of schools was a live question as early as the decade from 1890 to 1900. However, little or no attempt was made at transportation until the latter part of the decade, and then in only a few counties. The county superintendent's report from Duval County, included in the state superintendent's biennial report for the years 1898-1900, states that it was being planned to reduce the number of one-teacher schools from 45 to 15 three-teacher schools.

The concentration of these schools is accomplished by means of wagonettes, specially constructed for this purpose by the Board of Public Instruction. They are of such capacity as to carry 12, 14, 16, 18, or 20 pupils each. Twenty of these comfortable and commodious wagonettes are now running at an average cost of $20 each per month.

The same biennial report shows that the average length of term in Duval County at that time was five months. Assuming that the average bus carried 16 pupils, the annual per pupil cost of transportation was about $6.25. The report further states that the cost of building these wagonettes was about $75 each.

The minutes of the county superintendents' convention for 1902 contain the following:

Resolved 5. That we favor the consolidation of schools and to this end the transportation of reasonable numbers of pupils by school boards. We find that experience in at least nine counties of the state proves that such a system wisely administered results in better schools, better protection of isolated children, and a reduction of expenses. (Carried 24 to 3.)

An attempt was made by the state department of education in 1912-1913 to ascertain the cost and number of students being transported. The returns were incomplete, but $34,664.69 was reported as being expended by the several counties for transportation, which amount probably transported about 3,000 students.

Growth in School Transportation

The remarkable growth in transportation of school children in Florida for the past five years is shown in Table 14. The average annual increase of one year over another has been 38.4

per cent in total expenditures for transportation. The number of students transported has more than quadrupled since 1922.

TABLE 14

GROWTH OF TRANSPORTATION IN FLORIDA

Year	Number Transported			Total Expenditures for Transportation	Per Cent Increase of Total Expenditures for Transportation Over Previous Year
	White	Colored	Total		
1922–1923 ...	7,654	27	7,681	$249,685.65	
1923–1924 ...	11,899	25	11,924	293,284.73	17.5%
1924–1925 ...	15,900	27	15,927	506,411.24	72.7
1925–1926 ...	27,376	302	27,678	720,045.56	42.2
*1926–1927 ...	32,308	454	32,762	870,409.00	20.9
Average 38.3					

* These figures were secured from county superintendents' reports made to the state department of education and questionnaires mailed to the county superintendents.

The total current expenditures for white elementary and secondary public schools in Florida in 1926-1927 were $18,009,285. Of this amount, $863,467, or approximately 4.8 per cent, was spent for the transportation of school children. The portion of current expenditures going to transportation given in Table 11 ranges from almost nothing in some counties to practically one-fifth in several counties. Of the 32,762 children transported, 32,308 were white and only 454 were colored.

LEGAL ASPECTS OF SCHOOL TRANSPORTATION

A study of the essential features of laws concerning transportation of pupils was made by the Bureau of Education, Washington, D. C., in 1922 under the direction of Edith A. Lathrop, and published in *Rural School Leaflet No. 8*. It is stated in this report that all of the states have laws of one sort or another that make possible the transportation of pupils at public expense for consolidated as well as for other types of schools. County school boards in Florida transport school children at public expense by interpreting under an inclusive duty given them—to perform

All acts reasonable and necessary for the promotion of the educational interests of the county and the general diffusion of knowledge among the citizens. (Acts 1889, Chapter 3872, Sec. 20, Paragraph 11.)

There seems to have been little or no question concerning the legality of the expenditures of public money for the transportation of pupils even though it is not specifically mentioned in the Florida laws. This is not surprising for the legality of transportation had been settled many years before in other states. *Bulletin No. 6,* 1920 of the Massachusetts Department of Education states that in 1869 an act was passed in Massachusetts—

To authorize towns to raise and appropriate money for conveying pupils to and from public schools, the money so raised to be expended by the school committee at its discretion.

This was the first act specifically permitting transportation of school children at public expense.

A study of the status of school transportation was made in connection with the *State Educational Survey.* Questionnaires were mailed to each of the 67 county superintendents in Florida. Replies were received from 46 counties. The questionnaire made up in two parts was designed, first, to secure county summaries of policies, methods of transportation, numbers transported, administrative set-ups, etc. The second portion was planned to secure individual analysis of motor bus transportation of pupils. Copies of both are included in this study.

Total Expenditures

The total expenditures for transportation in the 46 counties reporting for the year 1926-1927 were $599,650, of which $594,695 was for the transportation of white children. The total expenditures for transportation for the state of Florida for 1926-1927 were approximately $870,409, and Table 11 shows that $863,467 of this was for the transportation of white children. Thus about 68.9 per cent of the state total expenditures for transportation of white children was reported in the questionnaires. The figures given in Table 11 for 1926-1927 will not be exactly the same as those which will be reported in the state superintendent's biennial report for that year. The figures given in the biennial report are taken from the annual reports sent in by the county superintendents. These reports are not made out uniformly. The figures given in Table 11 for 1926-1927 in this report are taken from these same annual reports, but corrected where questionnaire reports showed other more likely figures. For instance, counties, in reporting the total numbers transported in their

DATA ON BUS ROUTES FOR LOCAL DISTRICT

1. Number of district............
2. Area of district............
3. (*a*) Does district own repair shop and do own mechanical work?........
   (*b*) What was the initial cost of the shop building?..................
   (*c*) What was the initial cost of the equipment?......................
4. Is a regular mechanic employed or is a bus driver used part time?......
5. (*a*) Salary of regular mechanic.............. (*b*) Extra compensation allowed bus driver for work as mechanic.................

Note: Below special information is requested for each motor bus in service in the county. If bus is not owned by district, items 6, 7, 16, 17, 18, 19, 20, 21, 22, 29, and 39 need not be filled out. If the same bus is used on more than one route, fill out as if it were used on only one route except items 13 and 37. For these items, give the information separately for each route but in the same space. If the buses are insured all together under a blanket policy, record the data asked for all under Bus No. 1 and write the word "blanket" in the spaces for the other buses insured under this policy.

DATA ON INDIVIDUAL BUS ROUTES	Bus No. 1	Bus No. 2	Bus No. 3	Bus No. 4	Bus No. 5
1. Is bus owned by district?					
2. Make of bus					
3. Seating capacity of bus					
4. Is bus a remodeled truck or automobile? .					
5. Has the bus a closed or open top?					
6. Initial cost of bus					
7. Total annual cost of bus upkeep (gas, oil, tires, repairs)					
8. Average number of children transported .					
9. Number of miles of surfaced road on route (gravel, concrete, shells, etc.)					
10. Number of miles of unsurfaced road on route					
11. Is one round trip made daily per route? .					
12. Are two round trips made daily?					
13. Length of route, one round trip (out from school to end of route and back to school)					
14. How much liability insurance is carried? .					
15. What is the premium for the liability insurance?					
16. How much fire insurance is carried on bus?					
17. What is the premium for the fire insurance?					
18. How much accident insurance is carried on bus?					
19. What is the premium for the accident insurance?					
20. How much theft insurance is carried? ...					

DATA ON INDIVIDUAL BUS ROUTES	Bus No. 1	Bus No. 2	Bus No. 3	Bus No. 4	Bus No. 5
21. What is the premium for the theft insurance?					
22. Are gasoline and oil bought in quantity lots?					
23. Length of school term in days					
24. Age of present bus driver					
25. How many months has present bus driver been driving for the school?					
26. Number of accidents he has had resulting in death or injury to children or property damage					
27. Is bus driven by pupil, teacher, or someone not staying at school?					
28. Is bus driver man or woman?					
29. Yearly salary paid driver (fill this in only where bus is owned by the school)					
30. How much bond is required of bus driver?					
31. What does this bond cost?					
32. Does school or driver pay the cost of furnishing this bond?					
33. Is bondsman a local man or a surety company?					
34. Is bus driver employed for part or full time?					
35. If he is employed full time what are his other duties?					
36. If transportation is contracted for, what is the annual contract price?					
37. Is the contract open to competitive bidding?					
38. What time does it take bus to make one round trip (out from school and back) ...					
39. Estimated life of bus (number of years it has been in service, plus future service it has in it)					

FLORIDA EDUCATIONAL SURVEY

The Florida Educational Survey is making a study of the transportation of school children. The data asked for will prove valuable in the consideration of the problem of the consolidation of schools.

Will you help us by returning the completed report within one week after you have received this form?

GEORGE D. STRAYER
Director

County........... County Seat........................

County Superintendent.................................

STUDY OF SCHOOL TRANSPORTATION

(Data are requested for the school year 1926-27)

DATA FOR ENTIRE COUNTY	White	Colored
1. Average daily attendance of county		
2. Number of pupils transported Elementary		
High School		
3. Total expenditures for transportation per year		
4. Number of students transported by motor bus annually .		
5. Number of students transported by horse-drawn vehicles		
6. Number of students school pays parents to transport		
7. Number of students transported by trolley car		
8. Number of students transported by all other means		
9. Expenditures for transportation by motor bus per year ..		
10. Expenditures for transportation by horse-drawn vehicles .		
11. Amount allowed parents for transporting own children ...		
12. Expenditures for transportation by trolley car		
13. Expenditures for transportation by all other means		
14. Total current expense for all school purposes		
15. Number of one-room schools in county		
16. Number of two-room schools in county		
17. Total number of school buildings in county		

18. Number of cases of litigation since January 1, 1925, due to school children being injured while being transported...........

19. How many judgments have been rendered against the school board in these cases?............

20. How many cases are still pending in the courts?............

21. What is the sum total in dollars of the judgments rendered against the school districts in these cases?............

22. What part of these judgments was covered by liability insurance? (Give amount in dollars)............

23. How many children have been killed since January 1, 1925, while being transported by school authorities, due to (a) collision with trains .... (b) collision with other vehicles............ (c) overturning or leaving road............ (d) breakdown of bus............ (e) other causes............

24. How many children have been seriously injured since January 1, 1925, due to (a) collision with trains............ (b) collision with other vehicles............ (c) overturning or leaving road............ (d) breakdown of bus............ (e) other causes............

25. What is the present value of all the motor buses owned by the school in the county?............. Horse-drawn vehicles?............

26. What is the total amount of accident insurance carried on buses? ....

27. What damage to buses, caused by accident, has been suffered since January 1, 1925?............. How much of it was covered by insurance?............

28. What is the total amount of fire insurance carried on buses?...........

29. What damage to buses caused by fire has been suffered since January 1, 1925............ How much of it was covered by insurance?........

30. How much theft insurance is carried on buses?............

31. What loss by theft has been suffered since January 1, 1925?............ What part of it was covered by insurance?............

32. What is the rate paid per $1,000 for (a) liability insurance............ (b) accident............ (c) fire............ (d) theft............?

33. What is the total annual cost to the county of (a) liability insurance .... (b) accident............. (c) fire............. (d) theft............?

34. How many motor buses are owned by the county?............

35. How many are contracted for by the county?............

36. How many horse-drawn vehicles are owned?............. Contracted for............?

37. Check the distances elementary children must live from school before transportation is provided by school (a) over five miles............. (b) over four miles............ (c) over three miles............ (d) over two and one half............ (e) over two............ (f) over one and a half............ (g) over one............ (h) over one half............ (i) no transportation at any distance............

38. Under what conditions are high school students transported?.........

39. Check the following records kept for buses owned by the county (a) daily report of driver............ (b) record of gas, oil, and grease .... (c) report of repairs............ (d) tire mileage record .... (e) accident report form............. (f) other records ....

40. What are the chief objections offered to transportation in your county by parents?...... ....

41. Is county repair shop provided?......... Cost of building.......... Equipment............

42. How many shelters are provided children?................ Average cost............

43. How many mechanics are employed for the central repair shop of the county if one is provided?............ Total salaries................

44. What qualifications are required of bus drivers for school children? ....

(Please send blank copies of all forms used as records for motor buses. Include with these a copy of the rules and regulations for bus drivers.)

annual reports to the state department, did not include children whose parents were paid to transport them. In other counties, when total expenditures were reported, only that portion paid out of the county funds was included, the amount contributed by the local district being omitted. In other counties, where motor buses were bought by the county, the total cost of those buses was charged against transportation for that year, although the period of usefulness of the buses was probably nearer five years, and nothing was charged for the years following. The state superintendent's biennial report for 1926 shows per pupil expenditures for transportation as low as $3.76, $6.06, $7.93 and $8.58 in Holmes, Gilchrist, Santa Rosa, and Okeechobee counties, respectively. Dixie showed a per pupil expenditure of $86.84 annually. Studies of transportation costs in New Jersey, Connecticut, Alabama, and Pennsylvania indicate that the per pupil costs of transportation should show a fluctuation on the average of not more than the ratio of 2 or 3 to 1 passing from the sparsely settled counties to the more densely populated regions. Hence, the unusually wide fluctuations in per pupil costs shown in the biennial report for 1926 are likely due to lack of uniform reporting and accounting.

This conclusion was verified by a study of the questionnaires from those counties which reported. Consequently, the figures reported to the state department for the year 1926-1927 were changed accordingly. In studying per pupil costs of transportation, however, little attention should be paid to costs reported in countries transporting 100 students or less, because so few are transported that they are probably not representative of what transportation would cost in that county if done on a county-wide basis. So urgent is the need of uniform accounting and reporting for transportation in order to make just comparisons of costs and need for transportation that later in this report suggested forms will be set up.

NUMBER OF STUDENTS TRANSPORTED

Florida transported approximately 32,762 children in 1926-1927. Of this number, 32,308 were white and only 454 colored. The transportation of colored children is not yet general in Florida, but the state superintendent's biennial reports show it is increasing slowly. The questionnaire returns showed a total of 23,282 white children transported who were reported according to method of transportation. This is 72.06 per cent of the state total.

CHARACTER OF REPORTING GROUP

The expenditures for transportation for the counties reporting method of transportation in the questionnaire were $586,407, which is 67.91 per cent of the state expenditures for transportation. The per pupil cost of transportation for the questionnaire group is $25.19 and for the whole state $26.73. These differences are slight and could easily be due to lack of uniformity in reporting. A study of the counties reporting shows that they are scattered over the whole state. The transportation attempted varies from practically nothing in some counties to as extensive programs as are found in the state. A study of those counties not reporting shows approximately the same conditions. Thus it is fair to assume that conclusions based on a study of the questionnaires are valid within limits for the state as a whole as well as the reporting group.

METHOD OF TRANSPORTATION

The questionnaire returns from 44 counties reported the numbers transported according to the method of transportation. Those counties reporting were Baker, Bay, Bradford, Brevard, Broward, Citrus, Clay, Collier, Columbia, Dade, DeSoto, Dixie, Escambia, Flagler, Gadsden, Gilchrist, Glades, Hardee, Hendry, Hillsborough, Holmes, Indian River, Jackson, Lafayette, Lake, Leon, Madison, Martin, Monroe, Nassau, Oskaloosa, Okeechobee, Orange, Osceola, Palm Beach, Pasco, Pinellas, Polk, Putnam, St. Johns, St. Lucie, Seminole, Suwannee, Taylor, Union, and Volusia.

Of 23,282 white children reported, 94.65 per cent are being transported by motor buses, .29 per cent by horse-drawn vehicles, 2.98 per cent by the children's own parents, who are allowed public funds for transporting their own children, 1.99 per cent by trolley car, and .09 per cent by other means which is probably by boat or train. Assuming that the same percentages hold good for the whole state, of the 32,308 white children transported in 1926-1927, 30,580 were probably transported by motor bus, 93 by horse-drawn vehicles, 964 by parents who are paid by the school to transport their own children, 643 by trolley car, and 28 by other means. Of the 454 colored pupils reported, 424 are probably being transported by motor bus, and 30 by their own parents subsidized by the school. Thus, it is seen that practically all of the transportation of pupils in Florida is done by motor buses.

Thirty-seven counties distributed their expenditures for transportation according to the method of transportation. Of the total $524,914 so reported for both races, 97 per cent was spent for motor bus transportation, .30 per cent for transportation by horse-drawn vehicles, 2.66 per cent for transportation by parents, and .04 per cent for transportation by trolley car.

Studies Made in Other States Regarding the Relative Costs of Motor Bus and Horse-Drawn Vehicles

As has just been shown, horse-drawn vehicles at present are practically a thing of the past in Florida. Studies made in other states confirm the judgment of Florida school authorities in this matter.

In a report of the committee on school transportation problems in Massachusetts issued in 1925, the daily per pupil per mile cost of transporting pupils by wagons was found to be $.031 and by motor buses, $.014. This study was based on 3,514 children transported in 289 wagons and 19,106 children transported in 727 buses.

A study was made by the state department of education in Oklahoma of 33,369 students transported in 233 wagons and 923 motor buses in 1924-1925. The annual per pupil cost of transporting by wagons was found to be $16.18 and by motor buses $19.90. However, it was stated that the motor buses traveled longer distances and that the per pupil per mile cost of transportation by motor bus was less than by wagon. Data were not complete enough to make this calculation.

Other studies show little difference in unit costs. Again, it must be borne in mind that the wagons are probably operating over worse roads than the motor buses and that the motor buses are operating over routes in many cases too long for wagons. It must not be considered that the two methods are completely interchangeable. It might be advisable to furnish transportation by horse-drawn vehicles over some routes very difficult for buses to travel. Evidence, however, indicates that motor bus transportation is preferable where possible from every standpoint.

Distance Children Must Live From School Before Transportation is Provided

The distances both elementary and high school students must live from school before public transportation is provided vary in the different counties. Minimum distances range from 1½ to 3 miles for elementary students and 1½ to 20 miles for high school students. The median minimum distance for elementary students is 2.8 miles for the 42 counties reporting distances. Of the 22 counties reporting minimum distances for high school students, the median is 2.9 miles. Dixie County reports boarding high school students instead of transporting them. Gadsden County transports elementary students if old districts have been consolidated. Three counties—Palm Beach, Hardee, and Citrus —report transporting high school students if a high school is not located in the district in which they reside, and Volusia transports high school students if they live in a district which has been consolidated with another.

Records and Reports

Twenty-two of the 46 counties replying to the questionnaires reported that they are keeping some kind of regular records and reports. Most of the other counties probably enter the expenditures for transportation in the regular distribution ledger with no auxiliary records other than bills or vouchers and canceled checks. Only two counties, Broward and Pinellas, keep all of the following records: the daily report of the driver, record of gas, oil, and grease; record of repairs; tire mileage record; and accident report forms. These are considered as minimum essentials by bus operating companies. It must be borne in mind, however, that a different type of reporting is required if the district contracts for its buses. Seventeen of the 33 counties recording whether the buses were school operated or not, reported owning some or all of their school buses. Four hundred and eight buses were included in this report, of which 125 were owned by the school. Later in this report, a comparison of costs of the two plans of management will be made. Most of the counties reporting, which keep records, show an inadequate system. The majority keep two records or less, the most common being the drivers' monthly and daily reports. This makes cost comparisons difficult both within a county and among counties.

Objections to Transportation

The question addressed to the county superintendents was: What are the chief objections to transportation in your county? It was of a leading nature and likely to suggest isolated objections even where there were no serious objections. But even in that form, of the 41 counties replying, "no objection" was given thirteen times, and "not much objection" two times. By far the most common objection, which was stated twelve times, was that transporting small children for a long distance was uncomfortable for them. It would seem that overcrowded buses were largely responsible for this objection, for 8 out of the 12 counties reporting objections on this score also reported average numbers transported for some of their buses equal to or greater than the seating capacity, which would mean crowded conditions with attendant discomforts. Of the 28 statements made and listed as objections, 19 can be remedied by providing more and better buses. It would seem that the transportation of pupils who live an unreasonable walking distance from school is now quite generally accepted as a part of the educational program of Florida, and that the objections to it are not due to non-acceptance of it as a part of the program, but to details of management.

Personnel Study of Drivers

Thirty-seven county superintendents submitted qualifications required of school bus drivers. The three qualifications most frequently mentioned were that the driver must be sober, reliable, and 21 years of age. These comprise 57 of the 84 mentioned desirable qualities of a bus driver.

The ages of 232 bus drivers in 23 different Florida counties were reported. The median age is 35.9 years, and the average is 33.9 years. The range is from 15 years to 70 years. A distribution was arranged into four-year groups and the largest number in any one group is 43, which is the 15 to 18 years of age group. These are largely pupil drivers. The greater number of drivers seem to be grouped around the average age, however.

The average experience of 230 bus drivers in 1926-1927 in 24 counties was found to be 16.3 months. The average length of school term for the schools reporting for these 230 drivers for

1926-1927 was 164 days. Thus, the average term of service with the school of the 230 bus drivers at the opening of the year was only a little over two school years. This indicates that there is little permanency in employment for school bus drivers in Florida.

Most of the bus drivers reported are regular drivers who are not connected with the school. Of 326 drivers in 26 counties for whom this information was given, 249 were regular drivers, 72 were pupil drivers, and 5 were teachers. Where pupil drivers are employed, it seems to be in the interest of economy, for they can be secured for less money, and if a pupil lives on the outer end of the route, only one round trip need be made daily.

Salaries of Bus Drivers

Sixty-one bus drivers operating school-owned buses in Florida received annual salaries totaling $25,660, or an average monthly salary of $50.41. In a study made by the state department of education in Oklahoma in 1926, the data are given from which the writer calculated the average monthly salary of 1,155 Oklahoma drivers to be approximately $60.77 per month. The state department of education of Texas in 1926 reported an average monthly salary of $59.50 for 305 bus drivers. The average length of school term for the schools included in the Florida study was 167 days, in Oklahoma 163, and in Texas 160. In view of comparative living costs, Florida is paying her bus drivers rather poorly. However, the sample for which data were available is only about one-fourth of the state total of the district-owned vehicles, and it is wholly possible that if data for the whole state were available little difference with other states would be shown.

Accidents of Bus Drivers

In answer to the question: How many children have been seriously injured since January 1, 1925?—46 counties answering reported a total of 9 injuries from 7 accidents. Overturning of buses caused the injury of 3 of the 9 injured pupils, collision 1, and other unlisted causes 5. Accidents were reported in Volusia, Osceola, Orange, Madison, Jackson, Flagler, and Clay. Five bus drivers in the service of Osceola, Palm Beach, Jefferson, Volusia, and Jackson in 1926-1927 have had accidents resulting in injury to pupils or property damage. Three of the drivers are pupils, two are regular drivers, the ages are 55, 40, 20, 18, and 29 years, they are all men or boys, and they have had 9, 22, 48, 16, and 16 months' experience, respectively, driving for the school. The number of accidents is too small to draw any conclusions whatsoever as to the relation of age, experience, and sex to the number of accidents.

OWNERSHIP OF BUSES

School buses in Florida are owned by districts, by the county or by private individuals, and contracted for by the county. In a few cases, the school owns the bus body and the contractor the chassis. Of 320 buses reported in 27 counties, 235 were contracted for, 50 were owned by the county, and 35 by the special tax districts. It is estimated in Table 15 that there were 248 school-owned buses and 651 contracted for in the state of Florida in 1926-1927.

CONTRACT VERSUS SCHOOL OWNERSHIP OF BUSES

An attempt was made to determine the comparative cost of transportation by contract and school-owned buses. Inadequate accounting made it quite difficult to secure reliable data for this purpose. Information was available, however, for 61 buses operating in Lake, Pasco, Broward, Pinellas, St. Johns, and Volusia counties which are owned by the local district or county. In order to compute costs on a unit basis, the following information must be available: the initial cost of the bus, the length of the bus route, the average number of pupils transported, the length of the school year, annual salary of driver, annual cost of insurance, annual cost of upkeep and expenditures for administration. The total annual cost is arrived at by summing the last four items mentioned, plus one-fifth of the initial cost of the bus for depreciation, plus the interest on the investment. A bus will have some trade in value at the end of five years. In a continuous system of cost accounting, this trade in value can be subtracted from the initial cost of the bus and the difference recorded as the initial cost of the bus. In case a county repair shop is maintained, the cost of maintaining this shop should be included in the cost of upkeep. The final unit cost figure desired by which cost comparisons can be made perhaps most fairly is the cost of transporting one student one mile per day. This figure is arrived at by dividing the total annual cost

TABLE 15

ESTIMATED STATE TOTALS FOR BUS TRANSPORTATION, 1926–1927

Estimated total number of white students transported by motor bus	30,580
Estimated number of buses in state assuming 34 students carried per bus	899
Estimated number of school-owned buses assuming they are 27.6 per cent of the total	248
Estimated number of buses contracted for by the school	651

by the average number transported daily; divide this quotient by the length of the school term and finally divide by the length of the route, one round trip. This is not a new technique, variations of it having been used in several other studies on transportation costs, some of which will be discussed later. It can be written in formula form as follows:

$$\frac{\text{Total Annual Cost of Transportation}}{1} \times \frac{1}{\text{Average Number Transported Daily}} \times$$

$$\frac{1}{\text{Length of Term}} \times \frac{1}{\substack{\text{Length of Route} \\ \text{(one round trip)}}} = \text{Cost per Pupil, per Mile, per Day}$$

Commercial transportation companies have computed their transportation costs in the unit form for years. The fallacy of using any other form of comparison is well shown in Table 2 of *Bulletin No. 205*—"Transportation Costs and Problems in Texas Rural Schools," issued by the State Department of Education, Austin, Texas, in 1926. In that table, several cost comparisons were given and the final one arrived at was the average cost per child per month. It was found to be $2.48 for district-owned buses and $2.80 for contracted buses. Thus the contracted buses were represented to cost 12.9 per cent higher on this basis. The writer computed the daily per pupil per mile cost from data furnished in this same table and found it to be $.0052 for district-owned buses and $.0075 for contracted buses. The contracted buses were actually costing 44 per cent more on a true unit basis than the district-owned buses.

It must be borne in mind that the length of one round trip, regardless of how many trips are made, will be the denominator of the last factor in the formula. Table 16 shows that the average cost per pupil per mile per day of transporting children in 61 school-owned buses in Florida for 1926-1927 was $.0094.

Information concerning costs of transportation by the contract method was available for 160 buses operating in 18 different Florida counties in 1926-1927. Cost accounting for contract transportation is relatively simple. The information needed is average number of students transported daily, length of route, length of school term, contract price, and cost of driver's bond and insurance if the school pays that expense. In Florida, the contractor generally pays that expense and it is included in the contract price. The formula for computing the cost is the same as for school-owned buses. Table 16 shows that the cost per pupil per mile per day for transporting school children by the contract method is $.0094, which is exactly the same as under the school-owned system.

An examination of the tabulated computations in Table 17 will make clear why cost comparisons in order to be fair must be computed on a unit basis.

If one would have computed only annual per pupil costs, annual cost per bus, and cost per bus per mile per day, he might have been led to believe that school-operated buses are more expensive. But school-operated buses transport children 22.4 round-trip miles per day on the average, while contract buses make 19.5 miles per round trip. The average number carried per bus in school-operated buses was 38 and in contracted buses only 30. The average length of school term in districts owning their buses was 177.6 days and in districts contracting for their buses it was 165.8 days. So, taking into consideration the number of children transported per bus, the distance transported and the length of time for which transportation was furnished, there was no difference in the cost.

It might be suggested that one group on the average provided better and more comfortable buses than the other and that this should also be taken into consideration. In view of the fact that larger loads were carried in the school-owned buses, probably larger and more comfortable buses were used. The explanation of the larger loads carried by school-owned buses as being due to more overcrowding is equally plausible and this would result in less comfort.

When considering the conclusions of this study, the inaccuracies of the original accounting must be borne in mind. Then, too,

TABLE 16

COMPARATIVE COSTS OF CONTRACTED AND SCHOOL-OWNED BUSES

County	Cost Per Pupil Mile	
	Contracted Buses	School-Owned Buses
Brevard	$.012	
Broward	.016	$.006
Collier	.033	
Escambia	.008	
Gadsden	.004	
Indian River	.011	
Lake	.020	.033
Leon	.010	
Madison	.009	
Monroe	.009	
Nassau	.015	
Oskaloosa	.010	
Okeechobee	.007	
Osceola	.014	
Palm Beach	.011	
Pasco	.014	.003
Pinellas		.012
St. Johns		.009
St. Lucie	.009	
Suwannee	.005	
Volusia		.011
Weighted Average	$.0094	$.0094

TABLE 17

TRANSPORTATION COSTS BY VARIOUS UNITS

Unit	School-Owned Buses	Contracted Buses
Average annual cost per pupil	$ 35.68	$ 30.75
Average annual cost per bus	1,343.00	912.00
Average cost per bus per mile per day	.350	.283
Average cost per pupil per mile per day	.0094	.0094

the numbers upon which it is based are small compared with the total number of buses in the state. It is estimated in Table 15 that there are 899 buses in Florida transporting white children. There are probably not over 13 buses used in the transportation of colored children. Thus the sample of 221 buses is only about one-fourth of the total number. However, capacities are given for 320 buses in Table 19. The average for this group is about 30 per bus, which is nearly the same as the average capacity for the smaller sample. The conditions for the whole state are probably approximately the same as indicated by this report. It is possible that the conditions of school transportation, as outlined in this report based on questionnaires, are better than for the state as a whole, because those counties doing the best job of transportation are probably keeping the best records and more of that group answered the questionnaires. Several of the counties carrying out large programs of transportation did not reply, probably due to the labor of filling out the questionnaire. The cost figures presented in this report for transportation by contract are probably more reliable because of the larger number of buses for which adequate information was available and because accounting is relatively more simple and more likely to be accurate for this kind of management. Elsewhere in this report evidence is given to show that the annual per bus cost of this sample group was $1,031, as compared with $909 for the rest of the state. This would indicate either that more accurate records are kept for the reported group and the actual total expenditures for the unreported group, not all reported to the state, or that the per bus cost is higher in the reported group. The errors in reporting costs to the state department are liable to be particularly large where the buses are school-owned. Taking these things into consideration, the difference in per bus costs is not enough to warrant a conclusion that conditions of the reported sample are very far different from the rest of the state.

Studies in Other States of the Comparative Costs of School-Owned and Contracted Buses

As is reported elsewhere in this report, a study published by the State Department of Education of Texas in 1926 indicated that it was considerably cheaper to transport school children in district-owned buses than in contracted buses. Not all the factors affecting cost were taken into consideration, but it was stated that wide ranges of costs were found in both groups. These fluctuations were undoubtedly largely due to causes other than administrative.

Superintendent H. E. Greene of Antonito, Colorado, made a comparative study of costs of district-owned and contracted buses in 92 schools in 28 Colorado counties, and reported his study in the October, 1926, issue of the *American School Board Journal*.

TABLE 18

TRANSPORTATION COSTS IN COLORADO

Costs by Type of Districts	District-Owned Buses	Contracted Buses
Median cost per child per day for schools in irrigated districts	$.170	$.180
Median cost per child per day for schools in dry-land districts	.226	.470
Median cost per mile per day for schools in irrigated districts	.170	.250
Median cost per mile per day for schools in dry-land districts	.150	.175

This shows a slight advantage in favor of district-owned buses. This study is of particular value because the dry-land districts are sparsely settled and the irrigated districts densely populated. Many factors associated with density of population affect costs, and data so separated give more reliable cost indication. Unfortunately, the per pupil per mile calculation was not made. It is quite likely that the costs, if calculated on this true-unit basis, would show little difference.

BOND REQUIRED OF DRIVERS

Of 27 counties reporting on this item, bond was required of drivers in only 8 counties—Leon, Osceola, Oskaloosa, Jefferson, Holmes, Volusia, Jackson, and Flagler. The amount ranged from $100 to $1,000, the average being about $500. In most cases, it cost nothing, the bondsmen being local men. In two counties, Leon and Holmes, the bond cost $7.50 per $500, the bondsmen being surety companies, and the cost of it was paid by the drivers.

Transportation Insurance

Transportation insurance is of the following kinds: (1) property insurance, as fire, theft, or property damage to buses caused by accident; (2) liability insurance, as insurance against accidental injury of the people carried or damage or injury to other people or property.

Liability insurance was reported as being carried in Pinellas, Bay, and Martin. Ten thousand dollars was carried on each bus at an average cost of $48 per $10,000. Accident insurance was reported as being carried in Bay and Pinellas counties. Fire insurance was carried in Bay, DeSoto, Indian River, Putnam, St. Johns, and Volusia counties. Rates vary on fire insurance. Actual rates for different types of insurance were difficult to secure because several types of insurance are generally carried on the same policy. Theft insurance was reported in Pasco and St. Johns counties. School transportation insurance does not seem to be general in Florida.

Competitive Bidding on Contracts

A total of 21 counties reported on this item for 253 contracts. The average annual per pupil cost of transportation where contracts are open to competitive bidding was $31.92, and where they were not, it was $40.08. But when the daily per pupil per mile cost is computed, it is found in each case to be approximately one cent. As far as cost is concerned, there seems to be little to be said in favor of either practice, providing other factors mentioned elsewhere in this report influencing cost are the same for each group. If better service can be secured at the same cost by competitive bidding, it can be recommended on that ground solely. No data are available indicating the comparative types of service provided.

Depreciation of Buses

Eleven county superintendents estimated the average life of 122 school buses in their counties to be 5.3 years. The median is 5.1 years. This agrees with estimates made in other studies.

Time Spent by Pupils on the Road

A study was made of the travel time of 195 buses operating in 20 different counties in making one round trip. That time represents the total part of the school day spent riding on the bus by the child living at the farthest end of the route. The average for Florida was 86 minutes in 1926-1927, assuming this group to be a representative sample. The average length of route one way is about 13 miles. Children are not transported in most counties unless they live more than 2½ miles from school. Assuming that they are evenly distributed over the remainder of the 13 miles, the average child transported lives 7¾ miles from school and spends 51 minutes of the school day on the bus.

J. F. Abel, Assistant Specialist in Rural Education in the United States Bureau of Education, in 1924 found the median travel time in 222 consolidations to be 35 minutes, one way each day. That would be a total of 70 minutes spent on the road daily by the average bus as compared with 86 minutes for Florida.

MAKE OF BUS

By far the commonest make of school bus is the Ford. Most of the school buses are truck chassis upon which have been built bus bodies by local men. One hundred eighty-nine of 320 buses are remodeled trucks or autos, as reported in the questionnaires. Two hundred and nine are Fords, and 34 are Chevrolets. The tendency seems to be to buy the cheapest bus possible. It must not be inferred from this statement that this is a poor policy. Proper accounting over a period of time and further investigation are necessary before the size or price of the school bus, which will afford the most comfortable transportation at the most economical cost, is determined. The schoolman who is administering school transportation is constantly faced with the problem of arranging routes so that a maximum number of students can be picked up in a minimum travel distance. He is not always free to buy a predetermined standard, economical size motor bus. Only careful accounting in each administrative unit will determine definitely for that particular locality the most desirable type of equipment. However, the experience of other sections of the country will be of value to him.

INITIAL COST OF BUS

Information concerning the initial cost of 101 buses was secured from ten different counties. The average cost was $1,485 and the median $1,090. The median is the best measure of the central tendency because of the weighting effects of a few very high-priced buses.

CAPACITY OF BUS

A study of the seating capacities of 320 buses operating in 27 counties was made. The median size is 33 and the modal size 30. The mode is the best measure of central tendency here, for bus capacities are generally arranged in multiples of 5.

Bus Transportation reported in its February, 1927, issue that of 3,091 school buses built in 1926 in factories, 79.9 per cent were between 25 and 35 in seating capacity, 7.5 per cent less than 25, and 12.8 per cent more than 35. The seating capacity of 25 was the most common, 1,163 buses having that capacity. The next most frequent capacity was 35, a total of 561 being built of that capacity. It must be borne in mind that these are only the factory-built school buses. Most school bus bodies are built by local men rather than in factories.

UTILIZATION OF BUSES

It is of interest to note the extent to which the buses now in operation are daily carrying loads up to their full capacity. Table 19 shows that the total seating capacity of the 320 buses for which this information was reported was 9,651. The average total number carried per one trip was 9,494. Several buses make two trips, however, and these 320 buses with a seating capacity of 9,494 really carry on the average 10,879 children daily. If the use of a bus on one route is considered full utilization, some are being overused and the actual total utilization is 112.7 per cent. If the per cent of utilization is computed by dividing the total seating capacity by the average total number carried per trip, it is found to be 98.4 per cent. Either way it is computed, it can be considered high. However, too high a utilization figure might not be desirable if it is secured by overcrowding pupils so as to cause physical discomfort. In view of the fact that the average capacity of the buses was 30.1, the average number carried per bus per trip was 29.7, and the average daily attendance of Florida white pupils is 73 per cent of the enrollment, many of the buses must have been overcrowded at times in order to maintain so high an average.

TABLE 19

UTILIZATION OF 320 FLORIDA SCHOOL BUSES

Total capacity	9,651
Total average number carried daily per trip	9,494
Total number carried daily all trips	10,879
Per cent utilization considering one trip as full utilization	112.7%
Per cent utilization calculated on basis of average number carried per trip	98.4%
Average capacity	30.1
Average number carried per trip per bus	29.7
Average number carried daily per bus	34.0

TYPE OF ROADS OVER WHICH CHILDREN ARE BEING TRANSPORTED

Information on this item was furnished for 320 bus routes in operation in 27 different counties carrying an average daily total of 10,788 children in 1926-1927, which is a little over one-third of the state total. A grand total of 4,324 miles, one way, was reported for these routes. Of this total, 3,052¾ miles are surfaced and 1,271¼ unsurfaced. The percentages are 70.6 and 29.4, respectively. By surfaced road is meant gravel, concrete, shells, or any other material furnishing a hard surface for a dirt road. Unsurfaced roads do not present as severe a difficulty in the way of transportation in Florida as in many states, for many of the unsurfaced roads are sandy and do not get very muddy. Florida is at present completing an extensive road building program which will facilitate school transportation.

EXTENT OF TRAVEL BY PUPILS TRANSPORTED BY SCHOOL

The total miles of route were reported for 35.3 per cent of the estimated state total of 30,580 children transported by motor bus. Assuming that the average length of route is the same for the unreported portion, school buses are probably operating over approximately 12,250 miles of road one way per day. The questionnaires showed that 195 of 320 buses made one round trip daily and 125 made two round trips daily. The percentages of the total are 60.94 and 39.06, respectively. If one round trip is made daily, the actual distance the bus travels daily is double the length of the route one way, and if two round trips are made, the actual travel distance is four times the length of the route one way. Assuming these ratios to be the same for the unreported section of the state, 7,465 miles of the 12,250 miles total were traveled two times daily, and 4,785 miles were traveled four times daily, making a grand total of 34,070 miles traveled per day by Florida school buses in transporting white children.

Costs of Operating Buses

The total cost of operating 221 contract and school-owned buses in 1926-1927 was $227,843, which was approximately $1,031 per bus per year. The total cost of all transportation of white school children in Florida for 1926-1927 was $863,467. Of the 32,308 children transported, 30,580, or 94.65 per cent, were transported by motor bus. The probable total expenditure for motor bus transportation for 1926-1927 was 94.65 per cent of $863,467, or $817,272. This would make an average annual cost per motor bus of approximately $909. This would indicate that the sample from which costs of school-owned and contracted buses were contrasted was either more carefully reported or that the per bus costs of that group were higher. Both are likely to be partially true. The fact that costs were reported might indicate that more careful records were kept than in the non-reporting counties.

Estimating Costs for the State

The average length of school term in schools reporting transportation of pupils was 167.3 days in 1926-1927. The average length of school term for the whole state for white schools in 1925-1926 was 157 days. This is to be expected, as the consolidated schools which transport pupils have longer school terms on the average than the large number of one-room rural schools which drag the state total down. Assuming for the 899 buses carrying 30,580 white children in 1926-1927 a total of 24,500 round-trip miles daily (the total miles of one round trip are charged against all the children on the route for the entire distance in computing costs) for 167.3 days a year, the daily per pupil per mile cost of transporting pupils in Florida by motor bus for 1926-1927 was $.0065.

Transportation Costs in Other States

The state of Connecticut, as reported in the state superintendent's biennial report for 1925-1926, in that year transported 16,305 students at a cost of $621,397. The annual per pupil cost was \$38.11 as compared with an annual cost of \$26.73 per pupil for Florida for 1926-1927. The average daily per pupil per mile one way cost of transportation for Connecticut for that year was \$.0355. Dividing that figure by 2 to make it comparable with the figure for Florida, it is \$.0177. The correct figure for Florida probably lies between \$.0065 and \$.0094. Thus, transportation costs in Florida are quite reasonable compared with Connecticut.

Pennsylvania transported 48,194 children in 1925-1926 at a total cost of \$1,749,064. The annual per pupil cost was \$36.29. Alabama transported 31,198 children in 1926-1927 at a total cost of \$667,092 or a per pupil cost of \$21.38. Unfortunately, the daily per pupil per mile costs for these states are not available.

J. F. Abel, Assistant Specialist in Rural Education in the United States Bureau of Education, reported an average per pupil cost of \$32.55 for 22 states in 1922.

The per pupil per mile cost for transporting 9,026 children in 305 buses in Texas in 1924-1925 was calculated by the writer to be \$.0063 from data furnished in *Bulletin No. 205* issued by the State Department of Education in Texas.

The per pupil per mile cost for transporting 19,106 pupils in 727 buses in 1924-1925 was found by the Massachusetts Department of Education to be \$.014.

It must not be concluded from these figures that one state is doing a better job of transportation than another because it is getting it done for less cost. As has been indicated in this study, costs will vary in different localities regardless of the efficiency of management due to factors associated largely with density of population. Some of these factors are average distance a bus must travel to pick up a student, condition of roads, cost of living, and availability of public service facilities. Other factors which cause cost variations are type of transportation provided and extent to which the program is carried. By this last statement is meant that if a state transports only those students relatively accessible on good roads, costs should be lower than for a state which transports students who live in sparsely settled, inaccessible regions. When these factors are held constant, then cost variations which appear can be said to be due largely to efficiency of management.

ADMINISTRATIVE ORGANIZATION

A county system for the administration of transportation is proposed in Chart 1. Lines of responsibility indicate the county superintendent as the administrative head with the assistant superintendent in charge of business affairs, the superintendent

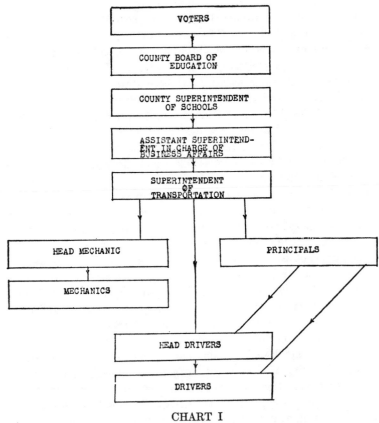

CHART I

ADMINISTRATIVE ORGANIZATION FOR SCHOOL TRANSPORTATION

of transportation, principals and drivers in the line organization in the order named. The head mechanic is a staff officer immediately responsible to the superintendent of transportation. The plan calls for a county repair shop and garages at the local schools. In case contract transportation is provided, the mechanic is omitted and the superintendent of transportation may be omitted also. Of course, in the smaller counties, the county superintendent will assume the line duties of officials not required because of small amount of transportation necessary. The contractor will be substituted for the head driver in case of contract transportation.

Among the Florida counties already approaching this scheme are Broward, Glades, and Pinellas.

Many advantages are to be had in administering transportation over a larger unit, either by contract or district-owned buses. Among those which are self-evident are collective bargaining, quantity purchasing, better opportunity for routing, and better accounting. Among those which are claimed, but which have not been thoroughly investigated due to inadequacy and lack of uniformity of records, are cheapness, better administration, and better service. A county-administered plan of transportation is in effect a merger of transportation lines which is the trend of commercial transportation.

Summary

1. Florida has recognized the legality of school transportation for over a quarter of a century.

2. The typical transportation conveyance in Florida is an overcrowded Ford bus, seating capacity 30, initial cost $1,090, body made by a local builder, driven 26 miles (round trip) daily in 86 minutes for 167 days of the year, by a man driver, 33 years old and having been in the service of the school about two school years.

3. Contract transportation is more common in Florida than transportation by school-owned buses, but there is little difference in the cost.

4. Little attempt is made at cost accounting for transportation. An adequate cost accounting system is recommended.

5. Administrative organization varies. A county administered plan is recommended with the county superintendent as the chief administrative head.

CHAPTER VIII

LIABILITY OF SCHOOL BOARDS FOR TRANSPORTATION ACCIDENTS

General Liability of School Boards for Their Torts

This question is tied up with the general liability of school boards for their torts or torts of their agents. Trusler in his book *Essentials of School Law* states:

> While it is well settled in respect to the personal liability of members of school boards for torts based on negligence that if the board as such is not liable, the courts have not excused them from individual liability for damages for torts that in a legal sense are legal and intentional, although such torts may be the direct results of their acts as a corporation.

He cites as evidence of this: (1) Bank *v.* Brainerd School District, 49 Minn. 106, 51 N. W. 814; (2) School Dist. *v.* Williams, 38 Ark. 454; (3) Adams *v.* Schneider *et al,* 71 Ind. App. 249, 124 N. E. 718.

Trusler also states:

> Under certain circumstances school officials may sustain a civil responsibility to persons injured by the mismanagement of school property. This liability may be either contractual or tortious; that is to say, it may arise either because of the breach of a contract or because of the breach of a duty imposed by law independent of contract. . . .

It is further stated in his opinion that a long line of American decisions exempts school corporations from liability for non-contract injuries inflicted by them, whether the injury be inflicted upon the person or property of the teacher, pupil, or any other person. State supreme court decisions, however, are on record conflicting with this statement, as will be shown later.

Robert C. Woellner commented in the April, 1927, issue of the *American School Board Journal,* on the unanimity of judicial opinion that school boards are acting in a governmental capacity.

He quotes from the famous Daniels case in Michigan,[1] as a typical case. The case concerned a boy falling over a faulty balustrade and sustaining serious injury. His parents sued in behalf of the boy, maintaining negligence on the part of the board. The court rendered a decision in favor of the defendant, maintaining that the school board was not liable because they were acting in a governmental capacity. The court also ruled that the board of education was empowered to raise money only for certain purposes and that those purposes did not include the raising of money to pay damages.

The writer of this report made a study of all superior court decisions that have been rendered in this country on the liability of school boards for torts, as reported in the *American Digest* from 1658 to September 1927. The number of cases in each state are given in Table 20. A total of 85 decisions has been rendered by higher courts up to September 1927. Six of these decisions were on school transportation. A bibliography of the cases is given at the end of this chapter. Some of these cases involve several decisions, for sometimes school boards have been sued as corporations and as individuals. Cases are on record of the city being sued when title to the school property is held in the name of the municipality rather than the school board. Court decisions, however, have been of the same trend regardless of who holds title to the school property. An example is: Hill *v.* City of Boston, 122 Mass. 344, 23 Am. Rep. 332. It was ruled that an action is not maintainable against a city for an injury sustained by a child while attending public school, through the unsafe condition of a staircase in a schoolhouse provided by the city, under a duty imposed upon it by public laws.

Of the 85 decisions rendered by the superior courts of the states, 2 of which were sustained by the United States Supreme Court, only 11 have been unfavorable to the school board or school board members. One of these decisions was later reversed. New York, Washington, and Michigan are the only states where higher courts have rendered decisions against school boards. Washington has since passed a law rendering the school board non-liable in certain cases. The tendency is to hold the school board non-liable unless statutory provision is made to the contrary.

A study made by Glen H. Kelley, reported in the February,

[1] Daniels *v.* Bd. of Ed. of the City of Grand Rapids, Mich., 191 Mich. 339; 158 N. W. 23.

TABLE 20

STATE SUPERIOR COURT DECISIONS ON TORTS
OF SCHOOL BOARDS OR SCHOOL BOARD MEMBERS (1658–SEPT. 1927)

State	Court Decisions on Torts of School Boards Other Than Transportation Cases	Court Decisions on School Board Liability for Transportation Accidents	Number of Decisions Unfavorable to School Board
Alabama			
Arizona	1		
Arkansas	1		
California	1		
Colorado	1		
Connecticut			
Delaware			
Florida			
Georgia	1		
Idaho			
Illinois	1		
Indiana	2	1 (1921)	
Iowa	2		
Kansas	2		
Kentucky			
Louisiana	1	1 (1927)	
Maine			
Maryland	1		
Massachusetts	5		
Michigan	1		1
Minnesota	2		
Mississippi			
Missouri	4	1 (1922)	
Montana			
Nebraska			
Nevada			
New Hampshire	1	1 (1904)	
New Jersey			
New Mexico			
New York	27	2 (1923) (1924)	8*
North Carolina			
North Dakota	2		
Ohio	4		
Oklahoma			
Oregon	1		
Pennsylvania	4		
Rhode Island	1		
South Carolina			
South Dakota	1		
Tennessee	1		
Texas	1		
Utah	1		
Vermont			
Virginia			
Washington	5		2
West Virginia	1		
Wisconsin	3		
Wyoming			
Total	79	6	11

* One case reversed decision.

1928, issue of the *American School Board Journal,* corroborates this statement. He states:

> Excepting New York, school districts are not liable for injuries to children received while being transported to and from school, through negligence of drivers or failure of the board to furnish properly equipped and guarded vehicles. Any duty of the school district to transport children to school is a public duty and the right to be so transported is a public right, so that in the absence of a statute making the district liable, action may not be maintained against it for personal injury to a pupil from its neglect by furnishing unsafe or unsuitable means of conveyance.

Perhaps this conclusion is a little too hasty, in view of the fact that only six suits on transportation torts have been reported. One of these, Williams *v.* Bd. of Trust., Dist. No. 1, Town of Eaton, 205 N. Y. S. 742, 210 App. Div. 161, was decided against the school board. A child was injured by falling from a platform spring wagon driven by a woman, which was the conveyance furnished by the school board. It was ruled that the school board in undertaking to furnish transportation must furnish a reasonably safe mode of conveyance and must also furnish a competent driver. It was ruled also that,

> Though the board of trustees of a school district is a governmental agency and, under Educational Law 270, is a body corporate, it is liable for its own negligence.

It must be borne in mind that even if a tabulation of decisions for and against a case shows a majority in favor of one side or another, the weight of evidence is not necessarily in favor of the majority of decisions. Decisions of courts in certain states influence judicial decisions over the country at large much more than courts in other states. The courts of New York and Massachusetts are among the most influential, and they take opposite stands on the question of liability of the school board.

In Ruling Case Law it is stated that school boards in England are quite commonly held liable for their torts.[2] The corporation, which is the local educational authority in that country, is liable for torts of school officials.

The question next arises: Are individual members of school boards liable personally for their torts? Trusler[3] states the following:

---

[2] Shrimpton *v.* Hertfordshire County Council, 104 L.T.N.S. 145, 75 J.P. 201, 27 Times L.R. 251, 55 Lal. Jo. 270, 9 L. G. R. 397, 48 Scot. L.R. 737, 2 N.C.C.A. 238.
[3] Trusler, Harry Raymond, *Essentials of School Law.*

Thus it has been held that school trustees are liable in ejectment or trespass for injuries to property in the conduct of their official business.[4]

Similarly it has been decided that for trespasses committed by school officers they are personally liable, and not the district.[5]

However, court decisions are conflicting on this point. In the case of Daniels *v.* Bd. of Ed. of City of Grand Rapids, it was ruled that, where a board of education is not liable for torts to pupils in its governmental capacity, its individual members are not liable.

In Ruling Case Law, Vol. 24, p. 606, it is stated that, as a general rule, the school board members are not personally liable for the negligence of their employees.

But a Board of Education having the management and control of the schools of the city, although not liable under the doctrine of "respondeat superior" for the torts of its subordinates, it is liable for its own participation in the wrongful appropriation of the property of another, and they may render themselves personally liable by negligence in the performance of duties to be performed by themselves. . . . But in regard to other matters all liability ceases when they employ proper persons to perform the work.

The following cases were cited: (1) Donivan *v.* McAlpin, 85 N. Y. 185, 39 Am. Rep. 649; (2) Wahrman *v.* Bd. of Ed., 187 N. Y. 331, 80 N. E. 192.

In the case of Bassett *v.* Fish, 75 N. Y. 303, it was ruled that "where a member of a board of education has been charged by the board as its agent, distinct from his corporate relation, with the duty of keeping the building in repair, he is individually liable for an injury occasioned by his neglect thereof."

Thus one finds conflicting decision after decision, but a distinct trend is indicated of non-liability of the school board in the performance of governmental duties, and liability of individual school board members if they assume executive responsibility.

As evidence that the matter of liability of school boards is still an unsettled question, the following headline was clipped from the March 1, 1928, issue of the *Charlotte Observer:*

$75,000 DAMAGE SOUGHT FOR GIRL'S DEATH IN SCHOOL BUS

The news item states that the Pender County, North Carolina,

---

[4] Bank *v.* Brainerd School Dist., 49 Minn. 106, 51 N.W. 814.
[5] School Dist. *v.* Williams, 38 Ark. 454.

school board was the defendant, charged with negligence. The following headline was clipped from an Alabama newspaper:

GIRL KILLED, 24 INJURED AS TRAIN HITS SCHOOL BUS

That is the customary way accidents in transportation of pupils occur. Years may pass before an accident occurs and then it is likely to result in wholesale injury. Of course the common-sense thing to do is to take all possible precautions, but despite this accidents will occur. Then the question of the moral responsibility of the school board presents itself. If a child is permanently incapacitated, through no fault of his own, by a commercial vehicle, corporation, company, individual, or by agents of the aforementioned parties, he has legal recourse and can recover. This is commonly accepted as right and just and accordingly liable parties are accustomed to protect themselves with proper insurance. If the offending party has no assets, the plaintiff has no recourse other than the pressing of criminal charges. If a child is so unfortunate as to be injured through the negligence of the school bus driver or through the negligence of the school board in providing an unsafe conveyance, it appears that in most states he has no recourse. This appears unjust, and probably dates back to the old monarchial period when the theory held forth that "a king can do no wrong."

Another legal question arising is: Has the school board the legal right to spend the taxpayers' money in order to discharge this moral obligation? Perhaps the answer to this question is that many school boards are doing it. Officials of the Aetna Casualty and Surety Company of Hartford, Conn., reported to the writer that their Company alone has over one thousand such policies in force. In a study made by the Massachusetts Department of Education, in 1925, it was found that 45 towns and one city were carrying liability insurance against injury of children while being transported. Eight cities and 66 towns report that liability insurance was carried by the bus drivers.

As evidence that the legal right of a school board to spend money in the discharge of its moral obligations is still doubtful, attention is called to a 1927 ruling of the attorney general of the state of Minnesota. He ruled that the board of education of School District No. 2, Lake County, Two Harbors, Minnesota, could not spend money for insurance against a liability which did not exist.

The next legal question which presents itself is: Since the school board is not liable in its corporate capacity, is it not possible that even though the school board does carry liability insurance the insurance company might refuse to pay damages on the grounds that the school board was not originally liable?

The committee appointed by the State Department of Education of Massachusetts for the study of school transportation in 1925 secured legal opinion on some of these questions. The conclusions reached were that the school board was not liable in its corporate capacity while acting in a governmental capacity, but that the school board members are liable in their individual capacities if they are wilfully and deliberately negligent. The opinion was also given that:

> The driver of the school bus is liable for injuries to children conveyed, whether the school vehicle is publicly owned or not.

The committee recommended that all school boards carry their liability insurance in the name of the driver and include the cost of such insurance as a part of the total compensation of the driver.

If the insurance is carried in the name of the driver, there may be no protection if a substitute driver is operating the bus in the time of an emergency. It would seem advisable to have the insurance contract so worded that the substitute driver will be included in the policy also.

The writer consulted with officials of the principal casualty and surety companies of Hartford, Conn., on this point. The leading companies are beginning to insert clauses in their policies waiving the right to refuse to pay the face value of the policy on the grounds of original non-liability of the school board. If the school board carries the liability insurance in its own name, this would seem to be a wise course to follow in order to avoid possible legal difficulties.

SUMMARY

1. Conflicting decisions are on record with respect to the liability of school boards in case of accident, but the general tendency is toward non-liability of school boards on the ground of performance of governmental functions.

2. Despite decisions to the contrary, school board members are individually liable for their torts in many states, when they assume executive functions.

3. Many school boards are carrying liability insurance despite the uncertainty of its legality.

4. The school board is undoubtedly morally responsible for the protection of children during transportation by adequate insurance, but there is still some question of its legal right to spend public money to discharge moral obligations.

5. If a school board carries liability insurance, one of the two following alternatives should be observed as a precaution in order to avoid possible legal difficulties:

   a. Carry the liability insurance in the name of the school driver and substitute drivers, including the cost of the insurance as a part of the driver's compensation.

   b. Require insurance companies to insert a clause in the insurance contract waiving their right to refuse to pay the claim on the basis of original non-liability of the school board.

BIBLIOGRAPHY OF CASES CARRIED TO THE SUPERIOR STATE COURTS OF THE UNITED STATES * (1658-1927) INVOLVING TORTS OF SCHOOL BOARDS AND SCHOOL BOARD MEMBERS

Arizona

1926 Sch. Dist. No. 48 of Maricopa Co. v. Rivera, 243 P. 609, 45 A.L.R. 762.

Arkansas

1822 Sch. Dist. No. 11 v. Williams, 38 Ark. 454.

California

1922 Solomon v. Red River Lumber Co., 206 P. 498.

Colorado

1925 Sch. Dist. No. 1 in City and County of Denver v. Kenney, 236 P. 1012.

England

Shrimpton v. Hertfordshire County Council, 104 L.T.N.S. 145, 75 I.P. 201, 27 Times L.R. 251, 55 Lal. Jo. 270, 9 L.G.R. 397, 48 Scot. L.R. 737, 2 N.C.C.A. 238.

Georgia

1925 Nabell v. City of Atlanta, 126 S.E. 905.

Illinois

1898 Kinnare v. City of Chicago, 49 N.E. 536, 171 Ill. 332.

Indiana

1895 Freel v. Sch., City of Crawfordsville, 142 Ind. 27, 41 N.E. 312, 37 L.R.A. 301.
1921 Union Traction Co. of Ind. v. Gaunt, 130 N.E. 136 (Ind. App.).

Iowa

1876 Wood v. Independent Sch. Dist. of Mitchell, 44 Iowa, 27.
1882 Lane v. District Tp. of Woodbury, 58 Iowa, 462, 12 N.W. 478.

* One case in England.

Kansas

1898 Rock Island Lumber & Mfg. Co. *v.* Elliot, P. 894, 59 Kan. 42.
1926 McGraw *v.* Rural H.S. Dist. No. 1, Linn Co., 243 P. 1038, 120 Kan. 413.

Louisiana

1927 Horton *v.* Bienville Parish Sch. Bd., 4 La. App. 123.

Maryland

1902 State *v.* Bd. of Sch. Com. of Frederick Co., 51 A. 289, 94 Md. 334.

Massachusetts

1860 Bigelow *v.* Inhabitants of Randolph, 80 Mass. (14 Gray) 541.
1877 Hill *v.* City of Boston, 122 Mass. 344, 23 Am. Rep. 332.
1879 Sullivan *v.* City of Boston, 126 Mass. 540.
1888 McKenna *v.* Kimball, 145 Mass. 555, 14 N.E. 789.
1901 McNeil *v.* City of Boston, 178 Mass. 326, 59 N.E. 810.

Michigan

1915 Daniels *v.* Bd. of City of Grand Rapids, 158 N.W. 23.
     Ferris *v.* Bd. of Ed. of Detroit, 122 Mich. 315, 81 N.W. 98.

Minnesota

1892 Bank *v.* Brainerd Sch. Dist., 49 Minn. 106, 51 N.W. 814.

Missouri

1899 Hydraulic Press Brick Co. *v.* Sch. Dist. of Kirkwood, 79 Mo. App. 665.
1921 Cochran *v.* Wilson, 229 S.W. 1050.
1922 Dick *v.* Board of Ed. of City of St. Louis, 238 S.W. 1073.
1925-26 Krueger *v.* Bd. of Ed. of City of St. Louis, 274 S.W. 811.

New Hampshire

1904 Harris *v.* Salem Sch. Dist., 57 A. 332, 72 N.H. 424.

New York

1861 Terry *v.* City of New York, 21 N.Y. Super. Cit. (8 Bosw.) 504.
1871 Allen *v.* City of Brooklyn, Fed. Case No. 218 (8 Blatchf. 535).
1871 Allen *v.* City of N.Y. Fed. Case No. 232 (17 Blatchf. 350, 5 Ban. & A. 57).
1877 Bassett *v.* Fish, 12 Hun., 209, reversed (1878) 75 N.Y. 303.
1877 Ham *v.* City of N.Y., 70 N.Y. 459, affirming (1874) 37 N.Y. Super. Ct. (5 Jones & S.) 485.

1878 Bassett *v.* Fish, 75 N.Y. 303.

1880 Donivan *v.* McAlpin, 46 N.Y. Super. Cit. (14 Jones & S.) 111, affirmed (1881) 85 N.Y. 185, 39 Am. Rep. 649.

1881 Donivan *v.* Bd. of Ed. City of N.Y., 85 N.Y. 117, Contra. see (1878) Donivan *v.* Bd. of Ed., 44 N.Y. Super. Cit. (12 Jones & S.) 53, 55 How. Proc. 176.

1881 Donivan *v.* McAlpin, 85 N.Y. 185, 39 Am. Rep. 649, affirming (1880) 46 N.Y. Super. Cit. (14 Jones & S.) 111.

1906 Wohrman *v.* Bd. of Ed., 97 N.Y.S., 1066, 111 App. Div. 345, affirmed 1907, 80 N.E. 192, 187 N.Y. 331, 116 Am. St. Rep. 609.

1907 Brown *v.* City of N.Y., 66 N.Y.S. 382, 32 Mis. Rep. 571.

1912 McCarton *v.* City of N.Y., 133 N.Y.S. 939, 149 App. Div. 516.

1917-18 Seel *v.* City of N.Y., 167 N.Y.S. 61, 179 App. Div. 659.

1920 Kelly *v.* Bd. of Ed. of City of N.Y., 180 N.Y.S. 796, 798.

1920-21 Jaked *v.* Bd. of Ed. City of Albany, 185 N.Y.S. 88, 113 Misc. Rep. 572.

1921 Jaked *v.* Bd. of Ed. of City of Albany, 189 N.Y.S. 697, reversing judgment 185 N.Y.S. 88.

1922-23 Herman *v.* Bd. of Ed. of Union Sch. Dist. No. 8, Town of Arcadia, Wayne Co. 234 N.Y. 196, 137 N.E. 24, affirming judgment (Sup. 191 N.Y.S. 930).

1923 Williams *v.* Bd. of Trustees of Dist. No. 1 of Town of Eaton, 198 N.Y.S. 476.

1924 Johnson *v.* Bd. of Ed. of City of Hudson, 206 N.Y.S. 610.

1924 Basnajian *v.* Bd. of Ed. of City of N. Y., 204 N.Y.S. 263.

1924 Williams *v.* Bd. of Trustees, Dist. No. 1, Town of Eaton, 205 N.Y.S. 742, 210 App. Div. 161.

1925 Basnajian *v.* Bd. of Ed., City of N.Y., 207 N.Y.S. 298, 211 App. Div. 347, reversing judgment (Sup.) 204 N.Y.S. 263, 122 Misc. Rep. 530.

1925-26 Katterschinsky *v.* Bd. of Ed. of City of N.Y., 212 N.Y.S. 424, 215 App. Div. 695.

North Dakota

1922 Anderson *v.* City of Fargo, 186 N.W. 378.

1922-23 Anderson *v.* Bd. of Ed. of City of Fargo, 190 N.W. 807.

Ohio

1874 Diehm *v.* City of Cin., 25 Ohio St. 305, affirming (1874) 5 Ohio Dec. 215.

1876 Finch *v.* Bd. of Ed. of Toledo, 30 Ohio St., 37, 27 Am. Rep. 414.

1905 Bd. of Ed. of Cin. *v.* Volk, 74 N.E. 646, 72 Ohio St. 469.

1923 Bd. of Sch. Dist. of City of Cin. *v.* McHenry 140, N.E. 169, 106 Ohio St. 357.

Oregon

1927 Spencer *v.* Sch. Dist. No. 1, 254, P. 357.

Pennsylvania

1881 Erie Sch. Dist. *v.* Fuess, 98 Pa. 600, 42 Am. Rep. 627.
1888 Ford *v.* Sch. Dist. of Kendall Borough, 121 Pa. 543, 15 Atl. 812, 1
  L. R. A. 607.
1907-16 Rosenblit *v.* City of Philadelphia, 28 Pa. Super. Cit. 587.
1923-24 Brinton *v.* Sch. Dist. of Shenango Tp., 81 Pa. Super. Cit. 456.

Rhode Island

1881 Mixon *v.* City of Newport, 13 R.I. 454, 43 Am. Rep. 35.

South Dakota

1913 Plumbing Supply Co. *v.* Bd. of Ed. of Ind. Sch. Dist. of Canton, 142
  N.W. 1131, 32 S.D. 270, modifying judgment on rehearing 142 N.W.
  260, 32 S.D. 129.

Tennessee

1927 (Shannon's Code, 1467).
  Johnson City Bd. of Ed. *v.* Roy, 289 S.W. 502.

Texas

1925 McVey *v.* City of Houston, 273 S.W. 313.

Utah

1919-20 Woodcock *v.* Bd. of Ed. of Salt Lake City, 187 P. 181.

Washington

1907 Redfield *v.* Sch. Dist. No. 3, in Kittitan Co., 92 P. 770, 48 Wash. 85.
1915 Howard *v.* Tacoma Sch. Dist. No. 10, Pierce Co., 152, P. 1004, 88
  Wash. 167, Ann. Cas. 1917 D. 792.
1918 Holt *v.* Sch. Dist. No. 71 of King County, 173 P. 335.
1920 Stovall *v.* Toppenish Sch. Dist. No. 49, 188 P. 12.
1926 Rice *v.* Sch. Dist. No. 302 of Pierce Co., 248 P. 388.

West Virginia

1925-26 Krutili *v.* Bd. of Ed. of Butler Dist., 129 S.E. 486.

Wisconsin

1918 Juul *v.* Sch. Dist. of City of Manitowoc, 169 N.W. 309.
1921 Sinka *v.* Joint Dist. No. 3, 182 N.W. 325.
1923 Sullivan *v.* Sch. Dist. No. 1 of City of Tomah, 191 N.W. 1920.

CHAPTER IX

COST ACCOUNTING FOR PUPIL TRANSPORTATION

Objectives of Cost Accounting for Transportation

I. A. May, in his book *Motor Bus Accounting Practice,* written for public service operating companies, gives the following reasons for cost accounting:

First, to know whether the rates of fare charged are commensurate with the services rendered.

Second, to find out, if possible, whether operating costs are as low as they should be, consistent with safety, and whether the greatest economy prevails throughout all departments.

Third, to find out whether it is better to manufacture and handle one equipment used in the service, or whether it is cheaper to procure it from an outside source.

Fourth, to serve as compass or guide so as to know exactly how the different machines are operating as to costs and how each department compares perhaps with the corresponding department of a similar company; also how the cost of operating one make of automobile compares with that of another or similar make.

Fifth, to furnish detailed information to support operating or financial statements of various kinds.

In the main, these could be assigned very well as reasons for a cost accounting system for public school transportation.

George Howard Jr., Director of School Organization, Department of Education, North Carolina, in an article in the June, 1925, issue of the *American School Board Journal,* in which he set up a simple cost accounting system for school transportation in North Carolina, stated:

It is maintained that no data should be required of principals or drivers except that which is needed and which has a direct bearing upon the superintendent's annual report. So in making up this system, this report is used as the basis and the other reports are suggested as the means of the superintendent collecting the information that is needed for his annual report.

This represents the common educational viewpoint of the function of cost accounting for pupil transportation, and the writer feels that it is weak in that it does not sufficiently emphasize the objective of better transportation at less cost, which is the principal end of cost accounting for commercial companies. It is so easy to collect general information or use estimated data rather than exact information, which looks just as good when tabulated and published in a report, that the irksome task of keeping accurate records on school transportation generally is not done by school men. Since the cost is paid by public taxation, competition does not force efficient operation. Commercial companies, on the other hand, are not concerned with publishing interesting summarized reports for public consumption, except as a matter of advertising. They are interested in being able to furnish better transportation at less cost to themselves than can their competitors. Consequently, commercial bus operating companies are far ahead of school operators in their accounting procedure. It is not a question of irksome labor to them, but, "Does it pay?" The answer has been that it is indispensable that the company keep accurate records if it is to be a profit-making concern. So important has it shown itself to be, that large commercial bus operating companies keep certified public accountants in their employ to make continuous extended cost analyses. It is not inconceivable that states, spending hundreds of thousands and some millions of dollars annually for school transportation, could well follow this example. It would be necessary to set up a uniform system of cost accounting for the whole state and cost analyses made over a period of years. There is no reason why a uniform system should not be adopted by all the states. Instead of commercial rivalry, good-natured professional rivalry among superintendents should stimulate them to bend every effort to provide the best transportation possible at the lowest cost for the pupils in their systems and thus add to their educational opportunity. This, of course, is impossible without comparable cost figures.

A progressive school administrator is constantly trying to measure and improve the efficiency of every unit of his system. The efficiency of many of his units, as, for instance, the efficiency of the instruction of a particular teacher, is difficult to measure, but it is being attempted nevertheless.

As an instance of this, consider the superintendent of schools who comes before his board and recommends that all the teachers should be four-year college graduates instead of two-year graduates. He states approximately the increased cost necessary to raise the standard of instruction. The question asked by the board and taxpaying public is: Will resulting increase in educational output justify the added expenditure? The superintendent has a difficult task, but he calls upon every available type of evidence. He appeals to logic. He quotes opinions of experts. He points out what other communities are doing. He arouses local pride. He gives what little objective evidence he possesses. He can afford to neglect nothing that will add weight to his case, so difficult is it for him to establish it objectively.

Contrast the situation which faces him when he presents his report on transportation, if he has been keeping adequate cost accounting records. In the first place, he can define adequate transportation. It is not good transportation or poor transportation. It is transportation in this type of vehicle or in that type. It is transportation in a motor bus of a certain size, closed top with glass windows, or with open top and side curtains, or a horse-drawn vehicle, or trolley car, etc. It is in terms of the understandable experiences of the board. If it is safe and comfortable, it is adequate. He presents his cost figures and shows comparatively how much transportation of different types costs. Then when he presents his program for the coming year and makes his recommendation, it is in terms of what kind of service a given number of dollars will buy.

The wise administrator, by taking advantage of every opportunity he has to justify the expenditures he recommends, breeds confidence in the administration and wins support for education.

So important has public transportation of school children become in the state of California that the California Taxpayers' Association interested itself in the problem of developing a uniform accounting system for transportation. They secured the services of P. P. Burch, former auditor of the Motor Transport Company, as an adviser to the Research Department of the California Taxpayers' Association coöperating with the Educational Commission of that state in the production of an accounting scheme reported in the September, 1927, issue of the *Tax Digest*. A Mr. Evans, working as a research student at the University of California, is at present making a study of transportation costs in California based on some 70 high schools which are using this uniform system.

Letters were addressed to all the state departments in the United States asking what studies on school transportation had been made in their states and requesting copies. Forty-two state departments replied. Of this number, Texas, California, Arizona, Wyoming, Utah, Minnesota, Nebraska, Oklahoma, Washington, Michigan, Illinois, Iowa, Arkansas, Alabama, North Carolina, New York, Pennsylvania, Ohio, Indiana, Maryland, Massachusetts, and Connecticut reported as having made one or more studies of transportation either in connection with a study of school consolidation or on transportation alone. Five states— Arizona, Washington, Michigan, Arkansas, and New York—are at present (1927-1928) undertaking studies on transportation. Practically all the state superintendents' biennial reports contain some data on school transportation in their states. Thus the general interest in the problem is apparent.

Suggested System of Cost Accounting for School Transportation

The writer, on the basis of an analysis made of these available reports, accounting schemes suggested and used in other states, accounting schemes used by commercial companies, and having made a detailed study of local problems of school transportation in Florida, worked out a suggested accounting and reporting procedure for school transportation in Florida which is believed to be practicable with slight modifications for other states. The aim of this study was not to turn out some new patented accounting system, but to put together meritorious parts of various systems now in use to furnish evidence necessary for the solution of transportation problems. Every item of data collected has for its purpose the objective of measuring something of importance in the efficient state and local administration of school transportation. The accounting system was developed primarily for the county unit type of organization, but no fundamental changes in the form are necessary for the use of states, with district, township, town, or parish units of administration. The only change in procedure is the officials who keep the respective records.

At first glance the accounting forms look somewhat complicated. They were made as simple as was consistent with adequate accounting control, however. It must be borne in mind that
when pupil transportation is entered into by the school, it
becomes a business and should be operated as such. When this
system is compared with the accounting system of commercial
companies, it will appear quite simple.

It is not intended that any one system keep all the records
presented. These records are designed for varying types of
organization, and one using them must select those suited to
his particular type of organization. In some systems, it might
be found desirable to consolidate some of the forms presented.
In an outline presented later, the indispensable forms are
indicated.

The aim in the development was to provide the same type
of information that commercial concerns find necessary, but to
state it in terms of educational accounting, which is intelligible
to the educator. The same type of classification was followed
as that used in the Uniform System of Educational Accounting
developed by Committees of the National Educational Association, and which is now in wide use. It was found possible to
develop the system in this fashion and still report unit costs in
the same units as commercial companies.

Different forms were developed for transportation by contract
and by school-owned buses. Provision is made in the accounting system for all types of transportation. It is not to be
expected that a cost accounting system will show for a state
that any particular type of transportation or type of administrative control is the best in every situation. It is not likely
that there is any one answer. Transportation by contract may
be the answer in one county and transportation by school-owned
buses may be the answer in another. One type of bus might be
more suitable for one locality, with its type of road and weather
conditions, than another. The only way to know is by a cost
accounting system which will give reliable, comparable data for
different situations in the state. It will not be necessary for
every county to experiment independently with a uniform accounting system operating. Two adjacent counties with comparable conditions using different methods of control or different
types of vehicles can compare costs. If they are using the same

methods or means of transportation they can compare themselves in efficiency.

An outline of a complete system of accounting is presented below for all types of transportation.

RECORDS AND REPORTS FOR TRANSPORTATION BY SCHOOL-OWNED VEHICLES

I. Records and Reports of County Office
  - *1. Contract
  - 2. Bond
  - *3. Annual Inventory and Record of Rolling Stock.
  - 4. Monthly Report of Superintendent of Transportation
  - *5. Annual Report of Superintendent of Transportation
  - 6. Driver Personnel Card

II. Records and Reports of Head Mechanic
  - 1. Daily Record of Head Mechanic
  - 2. Maintenance Program for Mechanics
  - *3. Annual Shop Inventory
  - *4. Stock and Equipment Record
  - 5. Tire Record
  - 6. Parts and Labor Record
  - *7. Monthly Report
  - *8. Daily Ledger of Expenditures**

III. Records and Reports of Principal
  - 1. Principal's Monthly Report
  - *2. Daily Ledger of Expenditures**

IV. Records and Reports of Drivers
  - *1. Drivers Daily Record
  - 2. Shop Work Order
  - 3. Accident Report
  - 4. Emergency Purchase Order

RECORDS AND REPORTS FOR TRANSPORTATION BY CONTRACT

*I. Contract
II. Bond.
III. Accident Report
IV. Driver Personnel Card
*V. Contractor's Monthly Report
*VI. Annual Report of County Superintendent's Office

---

* Records which constitute the minimum essentials of an accounting system.
** This record is to be kept by either the principal or the head mechanic according to the organization.

A form of each record and report is shown and a brief explanation made of its use. The records and reports for district-owned vehicles will be presented first.

Records and Reports for District-Owned Vehicles

Contract, Form 1. A sample contract is suggested in Form 1 similar to the form used by Montgomery County, Alabama, which has a well-developed system of county administration of transportation. It will be observed that rules and regulations are included in the contract. This is a growing practice among those administering transportation.

FORM 1

Transportation Contract

..........County Public Schools

..........County
State of Florida

This contract, entered into between the County Board of Education of ....County, the party of the first part, and..........
.....................the party of the second part, WITNESSETH:

1. That the party of the first part hereby appoints the party of the second part to a position in the Transportation Department of its organization for a term of.................calendar months, beginning.........
.................192............

2. That the party of the first part shall pay to the party of the second part............................. dollars, payable in monthly installments of........................... dollars each.

3. That the party of the second part agrees to perform services in this department under the direction of the County Superintendent of Schools, and Principal of...........................School.

4. That the party of the second part agrees to follow and enforce the following Rules and Regulations:

  a. A bus carrying school children must observe this procedure in crossing a railroad track: Stop 30 feet from the railroad track, have a student appointed by the principal for this purpose, get out and watch for trains until the bus has crossed the tracks. If the bus is empty the driver must come to a full stop, but need not get out.

  b. The driver must not leave the bus while the motor is running.

  c. Buses must run at least 75 yards apart on the road.

  d. Buses must be brought to a full stop before children are allowed to get on or off.

  e. Children must ride inside the bus and not on the outside of the body or in the driver's seat.

  f. No one except the driver and the children regularly assigned to the bus shall be allowed to ride on the bus without a permit.

FORM 1 (*Continued*)

g. Children shall have regular appointed places to get on and leave the bus. If the children are not present at that place when the bus arrives, the driver shall stop the bus until he has ascertained if they are in sight or not. If they are he must wait, but if not he shall proceed immediately.

h. The driver is expected to keep order on the bus. He must report daily all misconduct of pupils.

i. No driver will be allowed to substitute unless approved by the county office.

j. The driver must observe all road laws and regulations.

k. The driver must be neat in his personal appearance.

l. No driver shall partake of intoxicating liquors on a day he is driving, or smoke while he is driving the bus.

m. The driver must fill out all required records and reports.

n. The driver is responsible for reporting all mechanical defects of his bus.

5. That the party of the second part agrees to make bond in the sum of ....dollars, for the faithful performance of contract, said bond to meet the approval of the party of the first part.

6. That the party of the first part hereby reserves the right to annul this contract, and dismiss the party of the second part for incompetency, for inattention to duty, or whenever, in the opinion of the party of the first part, the best interest of the school service may require.

....
Party of the first part

WITNESS:

....
....

Approved by direction of the County Board of Education..........192....

....
County Superintendent of Education

Bond, Form 2. The following suggested bond form (Form 2) is similar to those at present in use in Volusia and Osceola Counties, Florida.

FORM 2

BOND

KNOW ALL MEN BY THESE PRESENTS, That we........................
of .... and.........
    Post Office   State
........................as sureties, are held and firmly bound unto the
County Board of Education of.........................County, State of
..............., in the full and just sum of.....................dollars,
lawful money of the United States, for the payment of which we bind
ourselves, heirs, executors, administrators, successors, and assigns, jointly
and severally, by these presents.

NOW, THEREFORE, THE CONDITIONS OF THE ABOVE OBLIGATION ARE SUCH,
That if the above bounden...............................shall faithfully
and truly perform a contract for the transportation of certain school
children of.........................County, ...State,
according to the manner therein specified and agreed upon and for the
consideration therein named, which said contract is hereto attached and
made a part hereof, and entered into this...........................day
of.................19.....between the said............and the County
Board of Education of......................County, ...
...............State, as required by law, then this obligation to be void,
otherwise to be and remain in full force and virtue.

IN WITNESS WHEREOF, The said...................................
and sureties have hereunto set their hands and seals this.............day
of.................19......

                    ....
                    ....
                                        Surety

WITNESS:

                    ....
                                        Surety

....

                    ....
                                        Surety

....
State of.................
.................County
Before me, ..., a Notary Public in and for............
County, ...State, this.....day of.................A. D.,
19......, personally appeared the said.................to me known and
known to me to be the individual who executed the foregoing bond, and he
acknowledged to me that he executed the same.

                    ....
                            Notary Public

FORM 3

Contract for Drivers of Contracted Buses

............County Public Schools

.................County

State of.................

This Contract, entered into between the County Board of Education of ....County, the party of the first part, and........ ...., the party of the second part,

Witnesseth:

1. For and in consideration of the sum hereinafter mentioned to be paid to him by the party of the first part, hereby contracts and agrees to perform the following described transportation of school children of........ ....County, ...State, according to the manner herein agreed upon and under the direction of the party of the first part.

....
....
....
....

2. The time of transportation shall begin on.................19....... and shall continue during the term of school at the option of the party of the first part. The party of the second part is to furnish, at his own expense, the above-mentioned vehicles, all necessary equipment, fuel, supplies, drivers approved by the County Superintendent of Instruction, and otherwise bear all expenses necessary to complete the terms of this contract without extra cost to the party of the first part.

3. The party of the second part agrees to make all reports required by the party of the first part.

4. (Here enter the same rules and regulations as are included in Form 1.)

5. For and in consideration of the services herein mentioned to be faithfully performed in accordance with the terms of this contract and in manner herein prescribed, the party of the first part hereby agrees and contracts to pay to the party of the second part the sum of.............. ....dollars, payable in monthly installments of................. dollars each.

6. That the party of the second part agrees to make bond in the sum of ....dollars, for the faithful performance of contract, said bond to meet the approval of the party of the first part.

....
Party of first part

Witness:

....

....

Approved by Direction of County Board of Education...........19......

....
County Superintendent of Education

ANNUAL REPORT OF SUPERINTENDENT OF TRANSPORTATION

COST ACCOUNTS	BUS NUMBERS																			TOTAL
	No.	No.	No.	No.	No.	No.	No.	No.	No.	No.	No.	No.	No.	No.	No.	No.	No.	No.	No.	
EXPENSE OPERATION																				
Gas																				
Oil																				
Grease																				
Batteries																				
Tires and Tubes																				
TOTAL																				
EXPENSE MAINTENANCE																				
Labor																				
Material																				
TOTAL																				
DRIVER SERVICE																				
Driver's Salary																				
FIXED CHARGES																				
Insurance																				
Bond																				
Rent of Buildings																				
TOTAL																				
ADMINISTRATION																				
Superintendent Transportation																				
Undistributed Overhead																				
TOTAL																				
DEPRECIATION																				
Rolling Stock																				
Repair Shop Building																				
Garages																				
Equipment																				
TOTAL																				
INTEREST ON INVESTMENT																				
GRAND TOTAL ALL COST																				
TOTAL MILEAGE																				
TOTAL NUMBER CARRIED																				
NUMBER ROUND TRIPS DAILY																				
NUMBER LOADS CARRIED DAILY																				
NUMBER DAYS OPERATED ON TIME																				
AVERAGE NUMBER CARRIED DAILY																				
COST PER PUPIL PER YEAR																				
COST PER BUS MILE																				
COST PER PUPIL MILE																				

Total Number Transported by Wagon..... Trolley ..... Parents ..... Other Means ..... TOTAL......

Total Cost Transported by Wagon..... Trolley ..... Parents ..... Other Means ..... TOTAL......

Total Number Transported by Contract..... Total Cost ..... Total Mileage .....

Number Contracted Buses ..... Cost Per Bus ..... Total Cost ..... Cost Per Bus Mile ..... Cost Per Pupil Mile .....

Grand Total Number Transported ..... Grand Total Cost ..... Average Daily Cost Per Pupil .....

REMARKS

Superintendent of Transportation

FORM 4

Recommended Size 14" X 17" Good Grade White Paper

FORM 4

ANNUAL INVENTORY AND RECORD OF ROLLING STOCK

Bus No.	Make	Number Cylinders	Seating Capacity	Initial Cost	Total Depreciation	Annual Depreciation	Present Investment	Number Years in Service	Final Disposal	Disposal Price
TOTAL										

FORM 5   Recommended Size 8½ X 11 Medium Grade Ledger Paper

EMERGENCY PURCHASE ORDER

No......
Issued to ......
Please supply the following to
the bearer and render invoice to
......Board of Education
showing this order number
......
......
......
......
......
Date..19....School .... Bus No.
                            Driver

FORM 6   3" X 6" Padded Book Form

MONTHLY REPORT OF SUPERINTENDENT OF TRANSPORTATION
Month Ending _____ 19___

Name _____   County _____

OPERATION AND MAINTENANCE	BUS NUMBERS																	TOTAL
	No.	No.	No.	No.	No.	No.	No.	No.	No.	No.	No.	No.	No.	No.	No.	No.	No.	No.
EXPENSE OPERATION																		
Gas																		
Oil																		
Grease																		
Batteries																		
Tires and Tubes																		
TOTAL																		
EXPENSE MAINTENANCE																		
Labor																		
Materials																		
TOTAL																		
STATISTICS OF OPERATION																		
Bus Mileage																		
Number of Round Trips Daily																		
Number of Loads Carried Daily																		
Total Number Carried																		
Number Times not on Time																		
Days Operated																		

Total Number Students Transported by Wagon ..... Trolley ..... Parents ..... Other Means .....   TOTAL ......
Total Cost Students Transported by Wagon ..... Trolley ..... Parents ..... Other Means .....   TOTAL ......
Total Number Students Transported by Contract ..... Total Cost .....

FORM 7   Recommended Size 8½ X 17 Good Grade White Paper

FORMS 5, 6, AND 7

Annual Inventory and Record of Rolling Stock, Form 5. If desired, this form may be part of the regular inventory of the whole school system rather than an auxiliary record. The information given in this form, however, is necessary regardless of where it is recorded. Some points about this form need explanation. The value of the tires and tubes on the bus when purchased should be subtracted from the purchase price and the remainder entered as the initial cost of the bus. The new bus is then charged with the price of the tires and tubes under the head of "Operation" in Form 12. Depreciation is computed as one-fifth the initial cost annually. The sum of the depreciation charges against a bus, plus the disposal price, minus the disposal value of the old tires on the bus at the time of its disposal, should equal the initial cost. If it does not, the depreciation ratio can be changed accordingly for similar buses in the future. The common practice is to charge one-fifth for depreciation. Some commercial companies subtract the disposal value of the bus from the initial cost of the new bus.

Monthly Report of Superintendent of Transportation, Form 7. This form is both a record and report and so a duplicate copy should be kept for permanent record. Maintenance and operation statistics are given in this report. It is possible to compute unit costs for every bus monthly from the data furnished on this report plus information furnished by other records of this system in the county office. The facts called for under "Statistics of Operation" may need explanation.

Bus mileage is the total number of statute miles traveled.

A round trip is concluded when the bus travels from the school to the farthest point on the route and back to school, or vice versa.

When a bus delivers a load of children to their destination it is recorded as a load. Thus a bus making one round trip daily makes two loads.

The total number carried is the sum of the numbers carried each load daily for the month.

The number of times not on time is the number of times the bus is a stated number of minutes early or late arriving at school, or at the homes of the children in the evening.

Days operated is the total number of days the bus carried children during the month.

Annual Report of Superintendent of Transportation, Form 4. This report is made out by the assistant superintendent in charge of business affairs if a transportation superintendent is not provided. In case neither is provided, the report is made out by the county superintendent of schools. This report which is also a record is a complete analysis sheet of all the transportation operations during the school year. Cost accounts are separated into a functional classification of operation, maintenance, driver service, fixed charges, administration, depreciation, and interest on investment. Educational authorities disagree as to the advisability of including the interest on the investment as a charge against education. Whatever can be said in its disfavor with respect to the school plant, in order to contrast costs of school-owned buses with contracted buses, is necessary, for the contractor certainly includes the interest on his investment in the bid he submits. The theory behind the imputed interest charge is that the money, if left invested in the community, would earn a return equivalent to the prevailing rates of interest in the community on long-term investments. The board rarely has the option of renting school buildings. It does have the alternatives in many instances of leaving the money in the community and contracting or investing in buses themselves. In contemplating district ownership, it seems quite fair that the interest on the investment should be made a legitimate charge against transportation by school-owned buses.

A duplicate of this report should be submitted annually to the state department of education.

The superintendent's statement of numbers of students of different ages living outside the minimum transportation distances for which state aid is allowed, in states using the scheme suggested in the first part of this study, should be submitted in his other reports from data furnished by the school principals.

There is not sufficient space on this form for a county with an extensive transportation program. Counties having more buses than can be reported on this form may use as many blanks as necessary and give the general data at the bottom and on only one sheet. If the county so desires, the horizontal length of the form may be increased as much as desired.

The item of insurance includes all transportation insurance on buses and children and insurance on garages and repair shops.

MONTHLY REPORT OF HEAD MECHANIC

For Month Ending _____ 19___

					Bus No.	Bus No.	Bus No.	Bus No.	Bus No.	Bus No.	Bus No.	Bus No.	Bus No.	Bus No.	Bus No.	Bus No.	TOTAL
ADJUSTING Valves Ground																	
Wheels																	
Brakes																	
Clutch																	
Springs																	
CLEANING Carbon																	
Motor																	
Body																	
GREASING Universal Joints																	
Transmission																	
Steering Gear, Springs																	
Fan, Clutch, Pump, Jackshaft																	
REPAIRS																	
NEW PARTS																	
Gallons Gas Issued																	
Quarts Oil Issued																	
Pounds of Grease Issued																	
Hours of Labor																	
Supplies																	
Cost Gasoline																	
Cost Oil																	
Cost Grease																	
Cost Labor																	
Cost Supplies																	
TOTAL COST																	

Total Cost Equipment _____ Supplies _____ TOTAL _____   Head Mechanic

FORM 8 Recommended Size 8" X 11" Good Grade White Paper

ACCIDENT REPORT

Bus No. ....   School ....Driver

Date .....19......   Time ....   Place ....

Kind of Accident ....

Speed of Your Bus .... Speed of Other Vehicle ....

Name and Address of Driver of Other Vehicle ....

Name and Address of Owner of Other Vehicle ....

What Laws Were Violated and by Whom? ....

License Number of Other Vehicle .... Operator's Number .... What Signals Were Given? .....

......................If at Night, Were Lights on Both Vehicles Lit?..................

What in Your Opinion, Caused the Accident? ....

....

Number of Students on Bus When Accident Occurred .... Make a Diagram on Back of this Blank of How the Accident Occurred

Names and Addresses of Other Witnesses:

PERSONAL INJURIES

Name   Address   Nature of Injuries

....

....

....

PROPERTY DAMAGE

Damage to Property of Others ....

....

Damage to Your Own Vehicle ....

Final Settlement:

FORM 9 Size 8"X 11" Good Grade White Paper

FORMS 8 AND 9

MAINTENANCE PROGRAM FOR MECHANICS

WORK TO BE DONE	Bus No.	Bus No.
ADJUSTING		
Brake		
Valves Ground		
Clutch		
Connecting Rod Bearings		
Wheels		
Spring Clips		
Steering Gear		
Body Bolts		
CLEANING		
Carbon		
Motor		
Body		
GREASING		
Universal Joint		
Transmission		
Steering Gear		
Fan, Pump		
Clutch, Jackshaft		
PAINTING		
OVERHAULING		
OTHER WORK		

FORM 11 Recommended Size 11" X 17" Cheap Buff Card

DAILY RECORD OF HEAD MECHANIC

WORK DONE	Bus No.	Bus No.	TOTAL
ADJUSTING			
Valves Ground			
Wheels			
Brake			
Clutch			
Springs			
CLEANING			
Carbon			
Motor			
Body			
GREASING			
Universal Joints			
Transmission, Steering Gear			
Springs			
Fan, Clutch, Pump, Jackshaft			
REPAIRS			
NEW PARTS			
Gallons Gas Issued			
Quarts Oil Issued			
Pounds Grease Issued			
Hours of Labor			
Supplies			
Cost Gasoline			
Cost Oil			
Cost Grease			
Cost Labor			
Cost Supplies			
TOTAL COST			

FORM 10 Recommended Size 8½" X 11" Medium Grade Ledger Paper

FORMS 10 AND 11

Under "Administration" the salary of the superintendent of transportation is divided according to the number of buses. Thus if a county has 85 buses, the charge against each bus would be one-eighty-fifth of the salary of the officer or officers administering transportation.

"Undistributed Overhead" is the difference between the sum of the mechanics' salaries and the total charge of labor under maintenance divided on a pro rata basis. In addition, the portion of time of any other school employee devoted to transportation services not otherwise distributed is charged under this item.

All salaries are taken from the regular payroll ledger of the school.

"Rolling Stock" refers to all buses and wrecking cars.

"Interest on Investment" is the interest at the prevailing rate on the sum of the present investment in rolling stock taken from Form 5 and the present investment in garages, shelters, repair shops, tools, equipment, and stock on hand taken from Form 20.

The "Cost per Bus Mile" is the cost of driving a bus one mile.

The "Cost per Pupil Mile" is the cost of transporting one student one mile.

Driver Personnel Card, Form 18. Commercial companies have found this information of value in selecting drivers. The qualifications necessary for a successful commercial driver are not so very far different from those desired in school bus drivers. It is believed that this information will be of value to the administrator.

Daily Record of Head Mechanic, Form 10. This record is necessary for analysis of operation and maintenance costs for each bus. If all buses are operated from the central shop, no record of maintenance and operation costs need be sent to the school principal and, consequently, those items will not appear in the principal's report.

Maintenance Program for Mechanics, Form 11. The head mechanic should work out his maintenance program for the whole year at the beginning of the school term. He should write the date in the appropriate square opposite each bus when the adjusting, cleaning, greasing, overhauling, and painting of each bus should be done. When the work is completed as the year progresses, he can check off the dates. The advantage of this type of a planned program is that work can be distributed equitably over the year and a glance at the sheet will show which buses need attention. Different makes of buses need a particular type of care at different intervals. The mechanic should obtain this information from the manufacturer and arrange his program accordingly.

Minneapolis represents an example of a school system which plans its entire maintenance program for all school property in this fashion.

Annual Shop Inventory, Form 20. This record is a part of the regular school inventory and can be kept as an auxiliary record or in the same binding with the complete school inventory of property. It is perhaps best kept as an auxiliary record and then entered in the regular inventory.

Daily Stock and Equipment Record of Central Repair Shop, Form 13. The head mechanic is charged with the goods he receives and this is his control account.

Tire Record, Form 21. A record of this kind is commonly used by commercial companies. An analysis of this sort will indicate the most desirable make of tire to buy.

Monthly Report of Head Mechanic, Form 8. This report is merely a monthly summary of Forms 10 and 11.

Principal's Monthly Report of Transportation, Form 12. This form, complete, is necessary when all supplies are not purchased at the central shop. In a large county it is more economical to keep supplies such as gas, oil, and grease at the garage in the local district. If the drivers use part of their time working on the buses in the local districts, this can be entered on this form. If all work is done and all supplies are purchased at a central shop, the driver's daily report should be submitted to the head mechanic and the principal need not make a maintenance and operating report. The only item that the principal need report, then, would be attendance of transported pupils.

Bus Driver's Daily Record, Form 16. This record is kept daily by the driver and submitted weekly to the principal or, if all buses are operated from a central shop, to the head mechanic.

Shop Work Order, Form 15. When a bus needs the attention of a mechanic, the driver fills out this form, ties it to the steer-

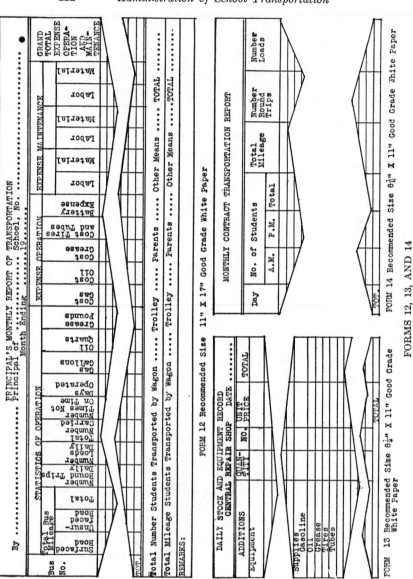

FORM 12 Recommended Size 11" X 17" Good Grade White Paper

FORM 13 Recommended Size 8½" X 11" Good Grade White Paper

FORM 14 Recommended Size 8½" X 11" Good Grade White Paper

FORMS 12, 13, AND 14

DRIVER'S DAILY RECORD

Bus No. .... Week Ending .....19..... School .... Driver ....

Number of Children Carried		Number of Miles Travelled on Regular Route	Number of Miles Travelled Not on Regular Route	Total Number of Miles Bus Travelled	Number of Gallons Gasoline Procured	Number of Quarts Oil Procured	Time You Left Going Out on Route	Time You Arrived at School	Did You Inspect Your Truck and Report all Trouble?
Morning Trip	Afternoon Trip								
Monday									
Tuesday									
Wednesday									
Thursday									
Friday									
TOTAL									

FORM 16 Recommended Size 5" X 6" Cheap Buff Card

DRIVER PERSONNEL CARD

Date ....

Family Name .... Given Name ....

Age .... Nationality .... Sex .... Married ....

Experience Driving Bus .... Schooling .... Do You Use Intoxi-
cating Liquor? .... Have You Ever Been Convicted of Crime? ....
What Physical Defects Have You ? ....
Where Were You Last Employed? ....
List References ....

FOR SCHOOL OFFICIALS

Date Employed .... Date Left Employ ....
Was Driver Discharged? .... If So, Give Reasons ....
Describe Accidents He Had, Giving Causes ....
Was Driver Satisfactory? ....

FORM 18 Recommended Size 4" X 6" Medium Grade White Card

SHOP WORK ORDER

Please make repairs on items marked "R" below and adjustments on items marked "A"

Motor		Gas System	
Brakes		Transmission	
Electrical System		Body	
Steering System		Cooling System	
Differential		Chassis	

Remarks:

Cost of Labor ..... Hours .....at $..... Per Hour $.......... Driver. ....
Cost of Materials ....
TOTAL $ ....
Date Completed .... Mechanic

FORM 15 Recommended Size 3"X 5" Cheap Buff Card

PARTS AND MATERIAL USED

DESCRIPTION OF PARTS	No.	Unit Cost	Total Cost
TOTAL			

FORM 17 Reverse Side of FORM 15

FORMS 15, 16, 17, AND 18

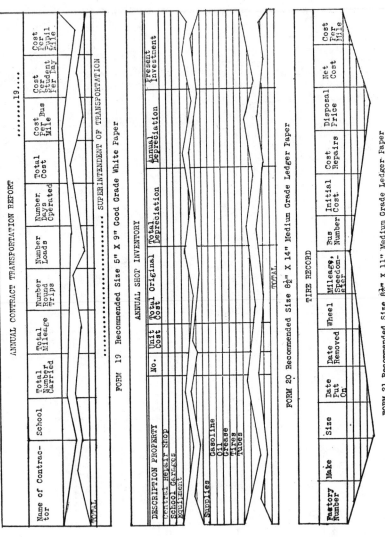

ANNUAL CONTRACT TRANSPORTATION REPORT ......19....

Name of Contrac-tor	School	Total Number Carried	Total Mileage	Number Round Trips	Number Loads	Number Days Operated	Total Cost	Cost Per Bus Mile	Cost Per Student Per Day	Cost Per Pupil Mile
TOTAL										

.... SUPERINTENDENT OF TRANSPORTATION

FORM 19 Recommended Size 5" X 9" Good Grade White Paper

ANNUAL SHOP INVENTORY

DESCRIPTION PROPERTY	No.	Unit Cost	Total Original Cost	Total Depreciation	Annual Depreciation	Present Investment
Central Repair Shop						
School Garages						
Equipment						
Supplies						
Gasoline						
Oil						
Grease						
Tires						
Tubes						
TOTAL						

FORM 20 Recommended Size 8½" X 14" Medium Grade Ledger Paper

TIRE RECORD

Factory Number	Make	Size	Date Put On	Date Removed	Wheel	Mileage, Speedom-eter	Bus Number	Initial Cost	Cost Repairs	Disposal Price	Net Cost	Cost Per Mile

FORM 21 Recommended Size 8½" X 11" Medium Grade Ledger Paper

FORMS 19, 20, AND 21

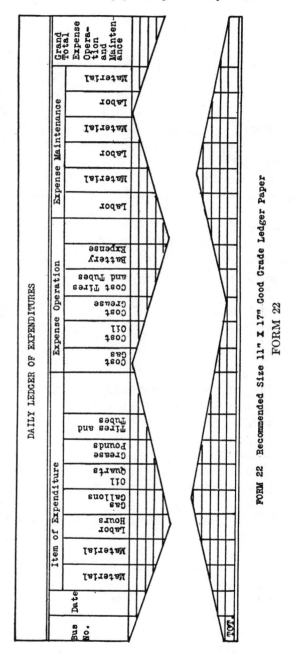

FORM 22   Recommended Size 11" X 17" Good Grade Ledger Paper

FORM 22

ing wheel, and leaves the bus at the repair shop. The mechanic fills out the reverse side (Form 17) and the driver takes it back to the principal when the job is completed. This is done in case all school buses are not operated from the central shop. If they are operated from the central shop, the head mechanic keeps the record.

Daily Ledger of Expenditures, Form 22. This daily record corresponds to a distribution ledger in any accounting system. It can be kept by either the principal or the head mechanic, according to the organization.

Accident Report, Form 9. This form should be filled out before leaving the scene of the accident and filed in duplicate with the principal. He keeps one and sends the other to the county superintendent immediately.

Emergency Purchase Order, Form 6. Frequently drivers find it necessary to make emergency purchases while on the route. If a systematic record is not kept, the accounting control will be difficult. It is made in triplicate, one copy being filed with the county office, another with the principal or head mechanic, depending upon the organization, and the driver keeps the third.

RECORDS AND REPORTS FOR TRANSPORTATION BY CONTRACT

Contract, Form 3. Many counties have found it advisable to include in the transportation contract a definite statement of the contractor's or driver's obligations and the rules and regulations deemed necessary and wise by the board of education. The contract suggested in Form 3 is not far different from those contracts at present used in Lake, Osceola, Volusia, and other Florida counties. Montgomery County, Alabama, has also been using a similar contract for some years. Form 3 is shown on page 113.

Bond, Form 2. The same form as is used with transportation by school-owned buses is satisfactory.

Accident Report, Form 9. The same form as is suggested for school-owned buses is satisfactory.

Driver Personnel Card, Form 18. It is recommended that the county office keep the same information on the contractor's drivers in the service of the school as is suggested for drivers of the school-owned buses.

Contractor's Monthly Report, Form 14. This record is to be kept daily by the contractor and submitted monthly to the county office.   The data asked for are stated in units comparable with data for school-owned buses.

Annual Contract Transportation Report, Form 19.   This is a cost analysis sheet developing unit costs comparable with costs for school-owned buses.   This should be kept filed as a permanent record.

It will be observed that cost analyses for motor bus transportation are emphasized in these records.   This is done because most school transportation is done in motor buses.   However, unit costs for other types of transportation are readily obtainable in this system.

CHAPTER X

SUMMARY—STATE AND LOCAL ADMINISTRATION OF SCHOOL TRANSPORTATION

Origin of the Problem

The transportation of school children at public expense has advanced from the status of non-inclusion in the legitimate tax program of the United States in 1869 to universal acceptance at the present time. Expenditures have mounted until in 1926-1927 approximately forty millions of dollars were spent for transporting 1,500,000 public school children. This growth has been due largely to the desire of the American rural people to provide an educational offering for their children equivalent to that of urban sections.

The principle of state responsibility for education has shaped itself into a very definite meaning in recent years. From a latent attitude of permissibility, the state has changed to an awakened attitude of conscious responsibility for the provision of equal educational opportunity for all children within the state. The definition of this attitude was brought to an objective focus by Mort,[1] who developed a technique for the accomplishing of this end by discarding the theory of state aid as a reward for effort and placing state support on the basis of a guarantee of a minimum educational offering to every child in the state, administered according to the ability of each community to support education, and its educational need.

The present study is concerned with one of those elements of need, namely, a factor beyond the control of the community, making necessary in some communities its inclusion in the school expenditures for the provision of an educational offering equivalent to that of other communities. Burns[2] developed a technique for measuring the transportation need of school communities and

[1] Mort, P. R., *The Measurement of Educational Need.*
[2] Burns, R. L., *Measurement of the Need for Transporting Pupils.*

128

suggested a plan for the administering of state aid for transportation. This plan had some weaknesses which rendered it impracticable for state-wide application.

STATEMENT OF PROBLEM

The first part of this study is devoted to the development of a new technique for the measurement of transportation need and the administering of state aid for transportation, taking advantage of the contributions made in Burns' pioneer study. The following standards were set up as the determinants of the validity of the scheme:

1. That the state should recognize the transportation being carried on in the average community in a group of communities whose needs for transportation are similar due to approximately equal effects of factors beyond the control of those communities, as the basis of the minimum program it will recognize in terms of numbers of students transported.

2. That the state should recognize, as the per pupil cost of its minimum program, the price paid by the average community in a group of communities whose costs for transportation are affected similarly by factors beyond their control.

3. That the state should recognize in its program of support the transportation done within the minimum determined by (1), and at a cost within the legitimate minimum determined by (2).

4. That state aid for transportation should not be distributed independent of the rest of the state's program of support, but should be combined with it and distributed on the basis of the community's ability to support education.

5. That the state in administering its program of support, while justly refusing to distribute aid on the basis of effort, should not by its administration of those funds encourage local inefficiency or extravagance or render the community inflexible to educational change or reorganization as the science of education progresses.

6. That if it is shown in the administering of the plan that communities by reason of factors beyond their control have a transportation need at variance with that predicted by the selected independent variable, or variables, that variation should be included in the minimum program.

The second part of the study is concerned with the development of a set-up for efficient local administration of school transportation.

PROCEDURE AND RESULTS

This first task was accomplished by (1), measuring the minimum program of transportation need in terms of per cent of the average daily attendance transported as related to the independent variable, average daily attendance per square mile. This procedure was validated by establishing a high association between the independent predictive variable and the variable to be predicted, by evidence from the states of Pennsylvania, Alabama, Florida, New Jersey, and Connecticut.

1. The function used for the prediction was the simple relation $\tilde{Y}_P = \dfrac{A}{X + K} + B$ where $\tilde{Y}_P$ is the transportation need as measured by per cent of average daily attendance transported and X, the independent variable, average daily attendance per square mile. It was shown that this function had properties rendering it capable of being fitted to the data of the five states used, and it is believed that it is applicable with certain adjustments to all the states.

2. The number of pupils in the minimum program was determined by multiplying the $\tilde{Y}_P$ value times the average daily attendance. The number of students for whom aid is to be allowed was determined by allowing the minimum program, if the community transported up to or above the minimum, and the number transported if it transported under the minimum.

3. The calculated cost of the program was found by determining the per pupil cost of transportation in the several communities due to the factors beyond the control of the community by the technique of correlations and regressions and multiplying by the number of students for whom aid is allowed. The validity of this procedure was substantiated by the establishment of high association between cost per pupil and average daily attendance per square mile from evidence furnished by five states.

4. The state aid allowed was determined by allowing the calculated cost, if the actual cost is equal to or above the calculated cost. The actual cost is allowed if it was below the calculated cost.

In computing the transportation expenditures within the minimum to be allowed each local district within a county to be counted in its total minimum educational program, the following procedure is suggested: If a county is transporting equal to or less than its minimum, allow each district all its expenditures for transportation. If it is transporting more than its minimum, divide the minimum program for the county among the several districts on the pro rata basis according to the amount each is spending.

5. State aid for transportation is to be distributed in combination with the other elements of educational need on the basis of the community's taxpaying ability. This is done by dividing the state aid allowed by the cost per weighted pupil as determined by Mort's technique and summing with the other elements of need.

It was found that different states had different minimum programs of transportation in communities of similar density. It is recommended that each state distribute aid on the basis of its own minimum program as being conducted consistent with its own educational organization, needs, and policies. This is discoverable by the fitting of the simple function $\tilde{Y}_P = \dfrac{A}{X+K} + B$ to actual percentages transported as related to density by the method of approximation or least squares.

A special study was made of local transportation problems in the state of Florida. This was done by the aid of the questionnaire and visitation. The results of this study are reported. An analysis was made of studies on transportation conducted by state departments, higher institutions, the United States Bureau of Education, and commercial concerns interested in bus transportation. On the basis of the status study in Florida, the evidence furnished by other studies and a study of the accounting practices of commercial companies, a cost accounting system was developed for public school transportation which it is believed lends itself to uniform application. This system was designed to make it possible to analyze transportation costs into the same cost units as commercial companies and to distribute the expenditures into functional headings similar to those used in the uniform system of educational accounting developed by committees of the National Education Association.

It is believed that this system will furnish the information for the local superintendent necessary for the efficient business management of transportation in his county. The reporting to the state department required of the local superintendent will furnish the state bureau of research with material to make significant studies on the business management of transportation. In addition, the state will have evidence necessary for the determination of whether local conditions beyond the control of the community justify a minimum program beyond that determined by the independent variables selected for the prediction of that need.

The liability of school boards in case of accident during transportation was investigated as a legal research.

In conclusion, it is not claimed that this study has opened up new fields for academic research. The researches suggested are the legitimate activities of the state department of research and local superintendents for practical use. No problems of local administration have been solved for all time. A successful solution to-day might be antiquated in the next decade. Partial answers to some are presented. Methods and means of arriving at the satisfactory solution of the more important problems are indicated. Finally, the state responsibility for a minimum program of transportation need has been objectively defined and a plan of administering state support for transportation is suggested, which safeguards the state against extravagance and mismanagement of the local communities and yet leaves the local community with freedom to expand, change, or exceed its present status in harmony with the advance of educational procedure.

BIBLIOGRAPHY

ABEL, J. F. "A Study of 260 Consolidations." *Bulletin No. 32, 1924.* United States Bureau of Education, Washington, D. C.

ABEL, J. F. "An Annotated List of Official Publications on Consolidation of Schools and Transportation of Pupils." *Rural School Leaflet No. 9, 1923.* United States Bureau of Education, Washington, D. C.

BURNS, R. L. *Measurement of the Need for Transporting Pupils.* Contributions to Education, No. 289. Bureau of Publications, Teachers College, Columbia University, 1927.

Bus Facts for 1927. Bus Division, American Automobile Association, June 1927.

Connecticut State Department. Report of Financing Education in Connecticut. Prepared by the Division of Research and Surveys of the State Board of Education, State of Connecticut, 1927.

ELDERTON, W. P. *Frequency Curves and Correlations.* Charles and Edwin Layton, London, 1927.

HAUER, R. and SCRAGG, G. H. *Bus Operating Practice.* International Motor Company, New York City, 1925.

HOLZINGER, K. J. *Statistical Methods for Students in Education.* Ginn and Company, 1928.

INDIANA. *Rural Education Survey Committee Report,* State Department of Education, Indianapolis, Ind., 1926.

MAY, I. A. *Motor Bus Accounting Practice.* Ronald Press Company, New York City, 1926.

MORRISON, F. W. *Equalization of the Financial Burden of Education Among Counties in North Carolina.* Contributions to Education, No. 184. Bureau of Publications, Teachers College, Columbia University, 1925.

MORT, P. R. *State Support for Public Schools.* School Administration Series. Bureau of Publications, Teachers College, Columbia University, 1926.

MORT, P. R. *The Measurement of Educational Need.* Contributions to Education, No. 150. Bureau of Publications, Teachers College, Columbia University, 1924.

NEULEN, L. N. *State Aid for Educational Projects in the Public Schools.* Contributions to Education, No. 308. Bureau of Publications, Teachers College, Columbia University, 1928.

REAVIS, G. H. *Factors Controlling Attendance in Rural Schools.* Contributions to Education, No. 108. Bureau of Publications, Teachers College, Columbia University, 1920.

SINGLETON, G. G. *State Responsibility for the Support of Education in Georgia.* Contributions to Education, No. 181. Bureau of Publications, Teachers College, Columbia University, 1925.

STRAYER, G. D. AND HAIG, R. M. *The Financing of Education in the State of New York.* The Educational Finance Inquiry Commission, Vol. I. Macmillan Company, 1923.

TRUSLER, H. R. *Essentials of School Law.* Bruce Publishing Company, Milwaukee, Wis., 1927.

YULE, U. G. *An Introduction to the Theory of Statistics.* Charles Griffin and Company, Ltd., London, 1927.